MISSISSAUGA YOUTH ANTHOLOGY VOLUME V

Ink Movement

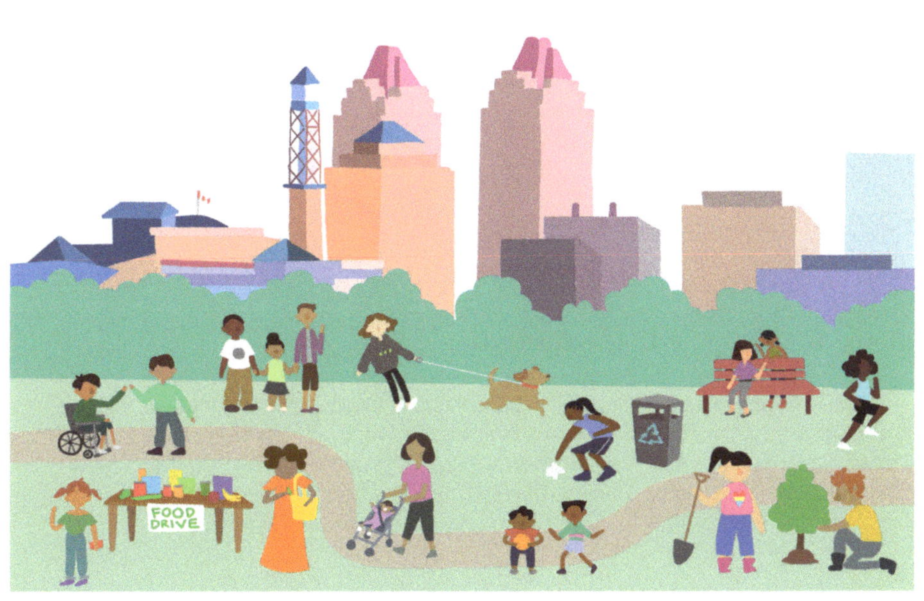

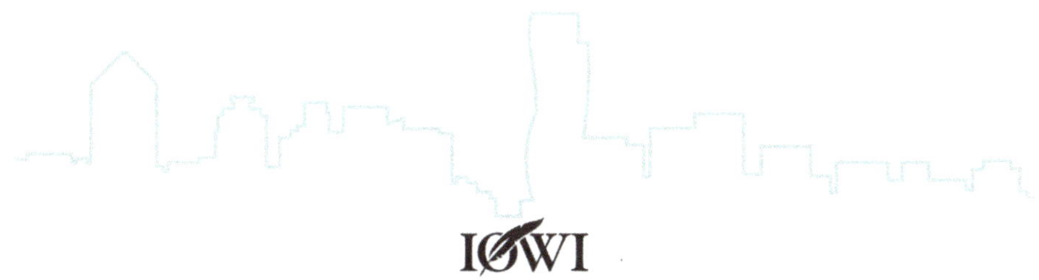

IOWI

MISSISSAUGA YOUTH ANTHOLOGY VOLUME V

Compiled by: Jacqueline Shi

Editors: Jacqueline Shi, Olga Nova, Khalisa Valani, Komal Patel

Cover Design: Tahreem Alvi, Sally Co

Inside Design: Shirley Aguinaldo
aguinaldo.shirl@gmail.com

Published by:
In Our Words Inc. /inourwords.ca / inourwords@bell.net
251 Queen Street South, Suite #561, Streetsville, ON L5M 1L7

Library and Archives Canada Cataloguing in Publication

Ink Movement's Mississauga youth anthology / compiled by Jacqueline Shi ; editors, Jacqueline Shi, Olga Nova, Khalisa Valani, Komal Patel

ISBN 978-1-926926-83-4 (v. 5 : softcover)

1. Youths' writings, Canadian (English)--Ontario--Mississauga. 2. Canadian poetry (English)--Ontario--Mississauga. 3. Short stories, Canadian (English)--Ontario--Mississauga. 4. Canadian poetry (English)--21st century. 5. Canadian fiction (English)--21st century. I. Shi, Jacqueline, editor II. Title: Mississauga youth anthology.

PS8235.Y6I65 2014 C810.8'09283 C2014-902636-6

Dear Reader,

I would like to thank you for picking up a copy of the Mississauga Youth Anthology: Volume V. Since November, the Ink Movement Mississauga team has invested an INKredible amount of effort into this publication. We are beyond excited to present to you the final product!

This year's Mississauga Youth Anthology focuses on "Community Development." Our goal is to showcase what empowerment means to the youth in our community, whether that be by volunteering in the community, solving problems with like-minded people, exploring their passions, or anything in between. We asked youth to take the Global Goals for Sustainable Development into consideration for some inspiration. We received over 100 unique submissions for the anthology, covering a wide range of art forms, ideas, topics, and styles. Our team worked together to organize the submissions and soon, bit by bit, the anthology began to piece together.

To the local youth who possess an endless amount of talent: thank you for taking the time to share your poetry, stories, art, and/or photography with us. Each and every piece of work that you have submitted contains passion and tells a story, which helps bring the anthology to life.

To the Global Youth Empowerment Fund: thank you for the endless support and with providing us with the funding for our publication, and feedback for our project. To In Our Words Inc., thank you for your hard work in proofreading and helping us produce such an amazing final product. To Jacqueline Shi, Olga Nova, Khalisa Valani, and Komal Patel: thank you for the hard work and passion you put into this anthology. To my fellow Ink Movement executives: I am beyond grateful for your commitment and love for team. Without all of this support, the anthology would definitely have not been possible!

Now I return back to you, reader. As you work your way through the writing, artwork, and photography, I hope you enjoy it as much as I do. What you want to do from there on is up to you. Perhaps you want to take a minute and connect the pieces of work to your own environment, tell your friends about it, or choose to take action and create a difference in your community. Whatever you decide to do, good luck on your journey!

On behalf of the entire Ink Movement team, thank you for your support towards our Anthology, and to the local youth artists.

Inkfam stay "ink"spired!

Uswa Zahoor

President
Ink Movement Mississauga

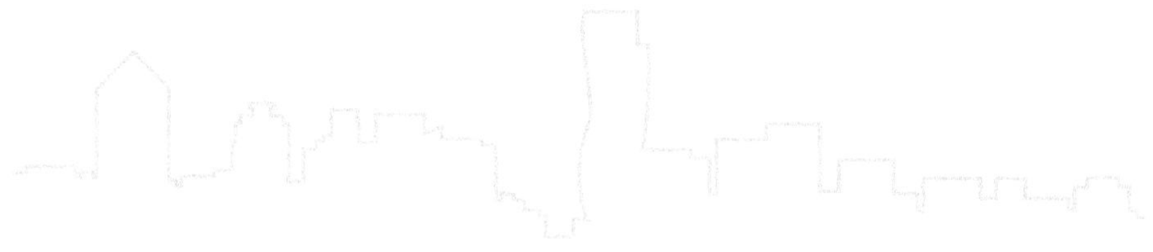

Dear Reader,

As with any anthology published by Ink Movement, the *Mississauga Youth Anthology: Volume V* is nothing short of exceptional. After months of planning and editing, we are thrilled to be launching the first coloured edition as part of the anthology series! This year's collection of poetry, prose, photography and art addresses the consequences and solutions to community issues such as poverty, gender inequality, lack of education, injustice and climate change.

Although we're living in one of the safest and most technologically advanced periods in history, there's no doubt that we continue to face social and environmental challenges on a daily basis. Luckily, this edition highlights ways to getting involved with organizations that are currently making a difference in the city of Peel, along with positive remarks from Mississauga's ward councillors regarding the importance of youth and the arts in our community.

As this year's project lead, I strongly believe that the anthology is more than simply a book consisting of pages held together by glue; it is an influential platform where youth are free to evoke social change in their communities through the arts and will continue to do so in the upcoming years.

I am incredibly thankful for all the inspirational and meaningful works submitted by the passionate individuals in our anthology, and can say that together, we are paving the way for a stronger and better community!

I would like to thank the Global Youth Empowerment fund and the Art Gallery of Mississauga for their continuous encouragement throughout the planning of the project. This anthology would not have been possible without their massive support! Thank you.

To the incredible Ink Movement team, thank you, Olga Nova, Khalisha Valani and Komal Patel for your contributions to the editing and planning of the anthology, as well as Cheryl Antao-Xavier for your supportive guidance throughout the assembly of the project. Thank you Maxwell Tran, for creating this amazing platform, and Uswa Zahoor, for your dedicated involvement throughout the year!

Lastly, I would like to thank you, reader, for expressing an interest in the arts and creative works published in our anthology. Art, as a medium, has the power to shape one's perspective and understanding of the world, and you are just beginning to embark on the journey.

Enjoy the ride!

Jacqueline Shi

Mississauga Youth Anthology Project Lead
Ink Movement Mississauga

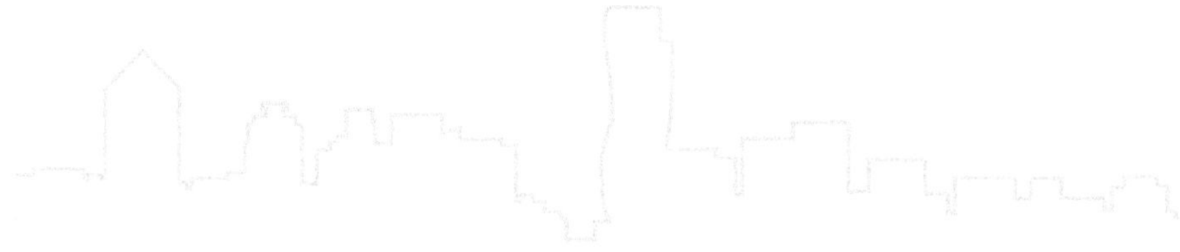

Dear Reader,

Thank you for embarking on this journey with us. We are thrilled to present Ink Movement's Mississauga Youth Anthology, Volume V! Can you believe this is our 5th book? (No? Neither can we.)

A lot has changed in the past five years. We've changed, you've (probably) changed, and so has the world. One notable change was the adoption of the Sustainable Development Goals by the United Nations – a set of 17 goals with 169 ambitious targets relating to health, education, poverty, climate change, and more. These "Global Goals" provide a foundation for us to work towards a more sustainable future, together.

Ink Movement has always been a socially conscious organization, so it was a natural fit for us to organize a youth anthology around the theme of sustainable development. More specifically, we wanted to know what 'Community' means to youth, and what they can do, or have done, to improve the communities they belong to. Which issues resonate with them? How have youth affected local and global, or 'glocal' change?

The submissions we received were impressive. Our team, as always, was amazed with the young artists in our city, and simultaneously honoured to showcase their talent to the world. Amidst all the negative attention that youth sometimes receive, we wanted to highlight the world-changers. The torch-bearers. The thinkers, doers, and dreamers.

No matter where you were born, what your native tongue is, or which god you pray to, the truth is: there is more that we have in common than separates us. And when we stand united in the face of wicked challenges in the world, we can conquer. Art – a form of expression that transcends borders, languages, and religions – happens to be our weapon of choice.

Enjoy.

Maxwell Tran

Founder and Executive Director
Ink Movement

CONTENTS

CONTENTS

MISSISSAUGA, A LOVE LETTER

Jordan Currie

This city let me use it as a blackboard.
This city let me look back,
look forward.
This city caught me with concrete arms when I fell,
echoed the whirring of my bicycle wheels
spinning in the stinging summer heat.
This city's frigid winters bit my cheeks
and frosted the car's windows,
bokeh lights from uniquely curvaceous Monroe-esque skyscrapers
behind the glass.
From the sizzling of eggs and rice my lola would fry in my childhood
mornings
to the walks to backyard playgrounds,
this city housed my work-in-progress soul
and no matter what, I could always count on it to lead me
right back to Square One.
This city gave me a childhood,
a liberty I, unlike so many unknowns
was granted.
This city is exactly that. A city.
A speck.
Like any other place where
the kids inhabiting its space had walks in the park,
playgrounds to climb on,
grandmothers to cook breakfast for them.
It's small here.
It does not seem like it when standing inside of its core
gazing up at its jagged skyline
but we're all sort of small, really.
Breathing, fighting,
trying to get from one day to the next.
This city has given me the chance to grow
into this obnoxious, evolving,

vastly-unpolished-tree-trunk of a girl.
If only others had the chance to grow as wide and obnoxious as me.
This city has given me opportunity.
Privileges.
I vow to use them to magnify those in positions less fortunate
in the ways I can summon. I owe this place that much.
This city fits snuggly in the palm of my heart.
This city has so many colourful faces.
This city is a speck
but community leaves footprints in the soul.
Mississauga,
you are not so much my anchor
but rather my dock,
raising me above the waves.
You are just like any other city
and thank you for being my dock.
My conventional speck,
my cosmopolis playground,
my root below earth.

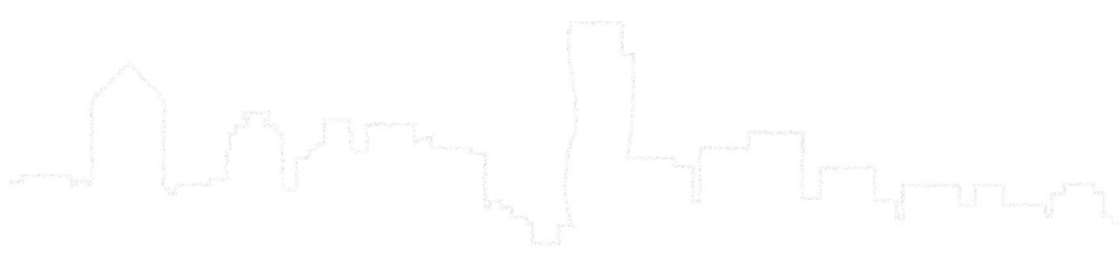

EXPLORING SAUGA 2

Jessica Chiong

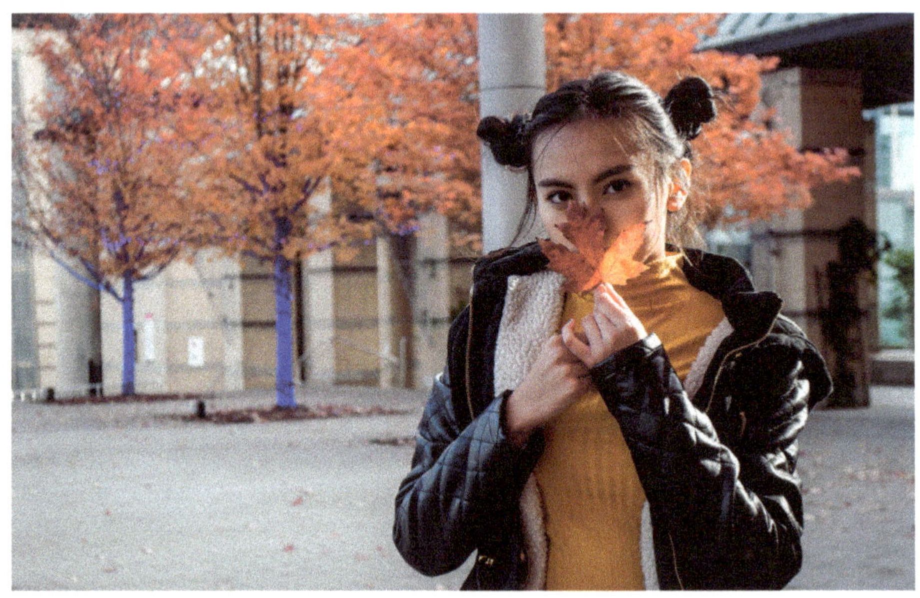

URBANIZATION

Jacqueline Shi

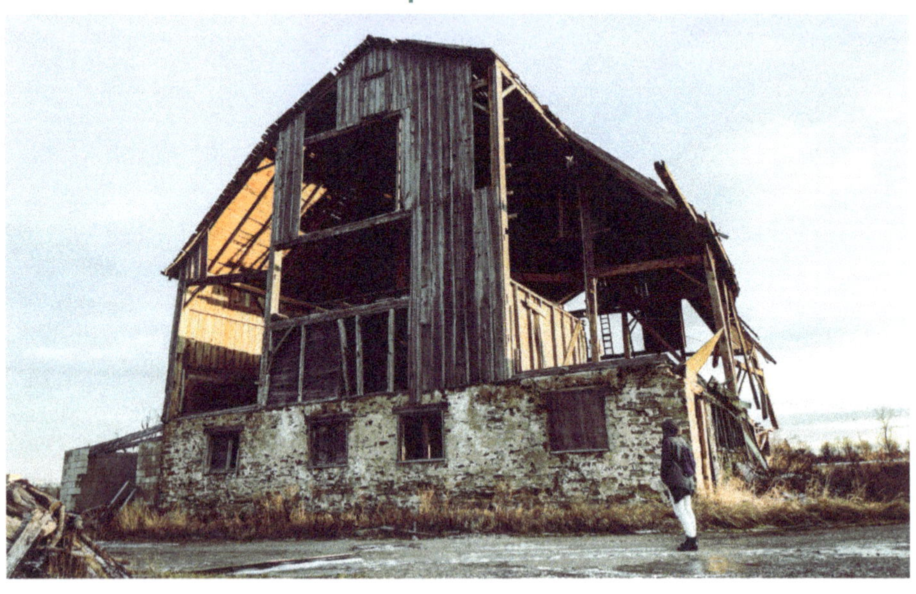

THE MAN WHO GREW FLOWERS

Sonya Zhang

They come around sometimes
and they claim they come with flowers
Pretty sparkly things to distract, to mislead, to hide -
her chubby arms and her big thighs
The flowers were so pretty
and the flowers were beautiful
but there was always a but-
Always a "What beautiful eyes but are you sure about those fries?"
Always a "I'm so proud but oh god her stomach is awfully round"
There was always a but-
So even though your flowers can take my breath away -
They were suffocating me
Even though you were only attempting to water them-
they are drowning

Because by the age of 15 I had learned the most flattering camera
angles and to hide behind things to appear smaller and to suck in
my stomach at the right time

I knew what pants would make me look 10 pounds lighter but never
what words to say to make myself 10 times happier
Because by the age of 15 I cannot write myself an honest love letter

So next time you come to grow your flowers I will ask you to leave
Because although your flowers are breathtaking and your flowers
are beautiful
I will learn how to grow my own

I will learn how to love each and every part of myself not in spite of
anything -
but because of everything
I will learn how to grow my own flowers

FROM THE ROOTS

Afrah Idrees

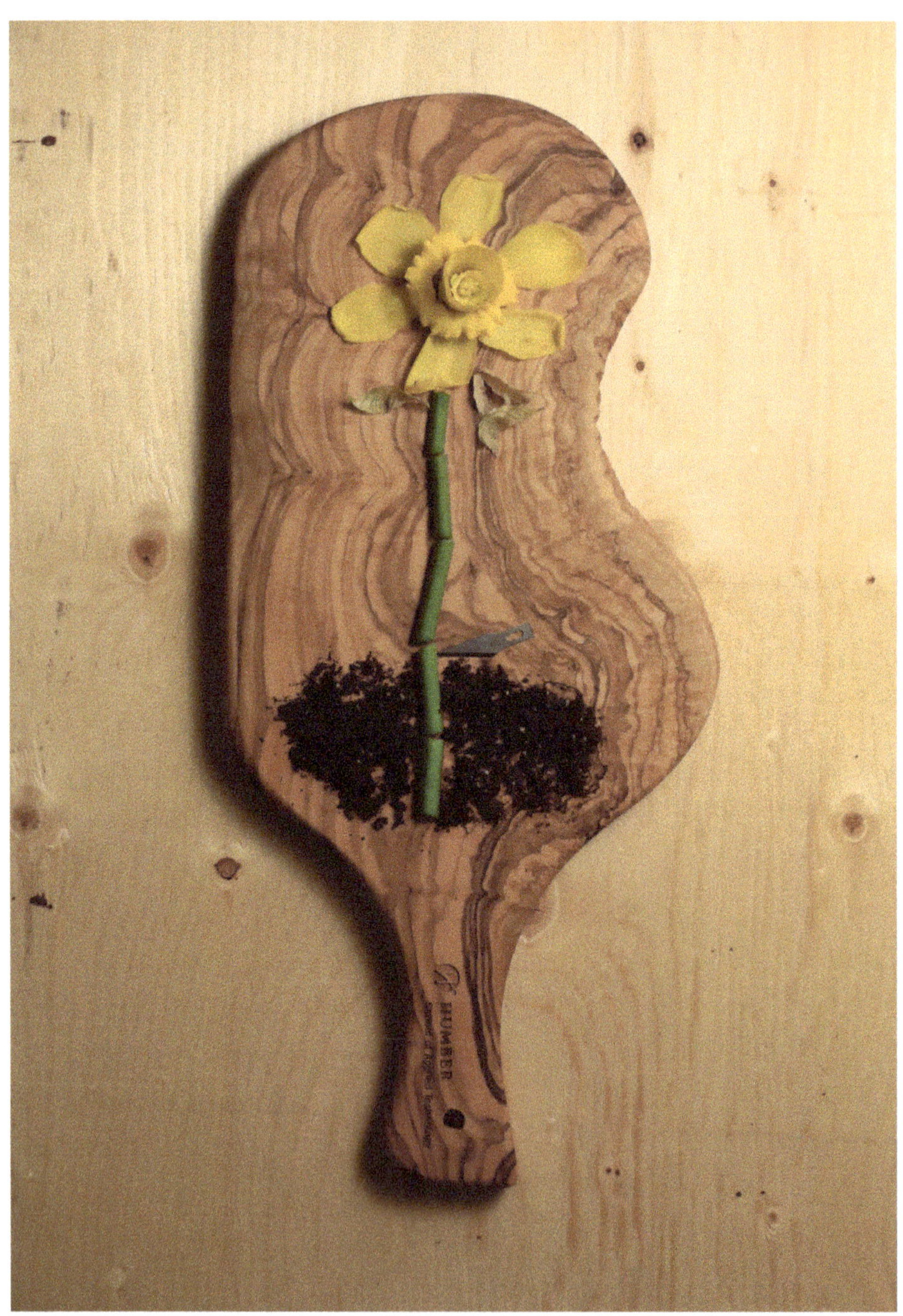

JACK FROST IS NEAR

Anthony Moss

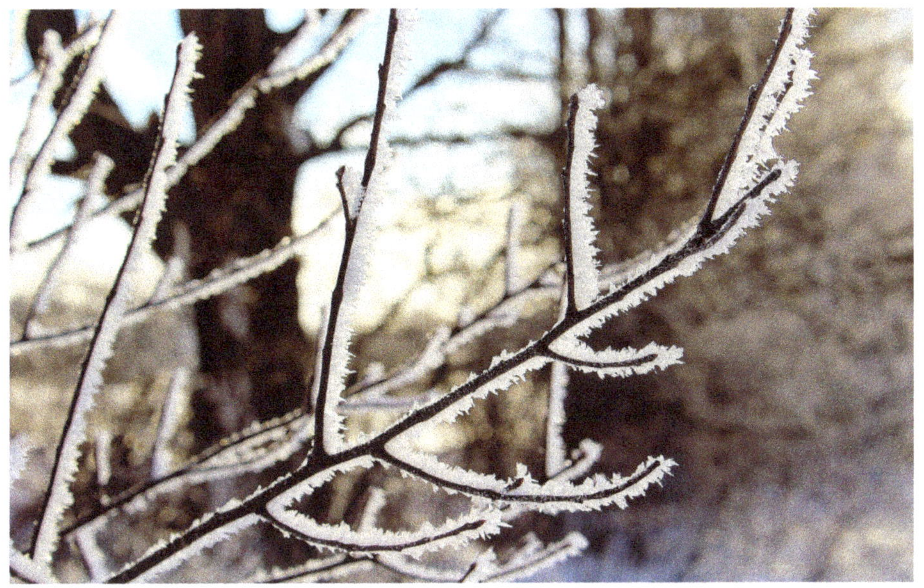

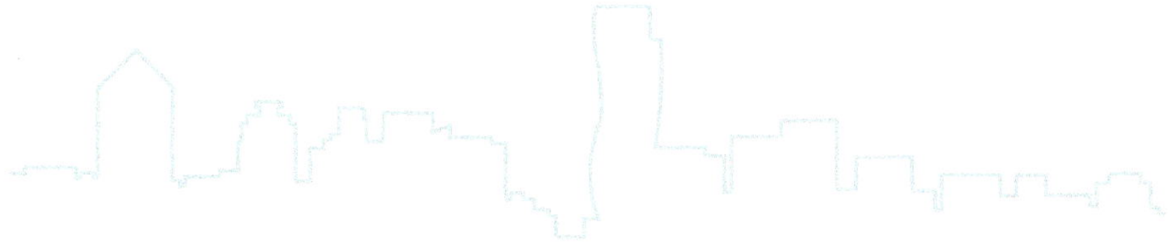

ABOVE AND BEYOND

Jesse Chang

"Finished."

I breathed out a sigh of exhaustion. The number of calls had been daunting, but they were finally completed. I sat back in my chair, satisfied with the day's work.

Satisfied. What a peculiar word. I only felt it once a day. Then, the worry of tomorrow settled in. Tomorrow, I would have to go to a board meeting and discuss the decrease in clients. My dry cleaning would be ready and needed to be picked up at noon, leaving only fifteen minutes for lunch. Then, Ms. Petal insisted we have coffee at six o'clock in the evening, so I would be awake the entire night.

I picked up my briefcase and walked out my office. After saying good-bye to the secretaries, I went down the packed elevator and let the crowd lead me onto the bustling sidewalk.

When I entered my house twenty minutes later, my butler, Ferguson, was readying the afternoon tea.

"Welcome home, sssir," he hissed.

Ferguson was a western taipan. His unique copper eyes fixed on me as he gestured at a table filled with warm biscuits, fresh melon, and Gruyère cheese.

"How wasss work?" he asked, pouring my tea with his tail.

"Fine. The company is having a problem with clientele, but my shares remain quite profitable. How about you?" I bit into a piece of melon.

"My day was wonderful! I cleaned your plaques and medals, washed the sheets, and visited the Lenons."

"Lovely. If you would excuse me, I should like a rest."

I walked to my room and lay down, staring upwards. The glass ceiling was one hundred metres above me, but I could see the orange clouds slowly turn purple. The surrounding walls darkened into a deep gray as the day drew to an end. The sunset casted its final rays on the wall with the staircase leading to the glass.

I thought about what my grandmother had told me about those stairs.

"Four hundred years ago, a strange poison had spread across the Earth, killing millions. Populations were forced into deep canyons which the toxins mysteriously evaded. These sites eventually developed into large cities with glass coverings overhead. This allowed heat and sunlight to pass through but kept the city dry and clean. As time moved forward, the air eventually cleared, but the people had no desire to return to the land above. They had become prosperous and comfortable."

"Then why do the staircases exist?" I had asked her.

"It is because the architect who designed our city wanted us to have a choice. We were not made to thrive underground; our place is up there, with the flowers and the grass, the moon and the stars. We have grown fond of many treasures here, but I believe true fulfillment is beyond them."

Ever since that conversation, I had wanted to venture to the world above. The sunlight was unbearably beautiful; I wanted to know what else accompanied it. However, I was afraid to be judged. It would be considered insanity to leave the city.

Another obstacle happened to be Ferguson. Every time I took a step up the staircase, he would be knocking at my door. His eerie presence would always frighten me, and the determination left as I let him enter.

"Well, tonight will be different," I had said to myself. "I am tired of being fearful. It is time to see the flowers."

* * *

It was around eleven in the evening when I crawled out of bed and crept to the staircase. After taking a step, I hesitated, waiting for Ferguson. There was no knock.

I took a few more cautious steps then began to run. After all, this was my sole opportunity to escape.

The climb seemed to take many hours, but my pace did not slow. I did not want to lose the strange urge that overcame me.

When I was only thirty steps from the top, I heard a hissing to my left. Ferguson had materialized at my side and was staring at me with those hypnotic eyes.

"I knew you were awake. For the past few monthsss, you have ssseemed troubled. What isss it, sssir?"

"Leave me be, Ferguson. I want to see the world above."

"Why? You are the wealthy presssident of an esssteemed law firm, and I wait on your every whim."

"That has never mattered to me. Part of me is missing, and I know it is somewhere beyond the city."

At this, Ferguson's eyes grew intense.

"Ssstay with me."

"No."

"Then I have no other choice but to make you ssstay."

With a sharp hiss, Ferguson opened his jaws, revealing fangs coated in deadly venom.

As his teeth met my skin, the moonlight suddenly glared brightly. A scream filled the night.

When my focus returned, Ferguson had disappeared. The moonlight was shining less intensely but seemed to be lighting the remaining portion of the staircase. The glass above the stairs had shattered.

I climbed the rest of the way and paused at the top.

The sight was breathtaking: a meadow with a pristine pond in the center. The moon and the stars lighted the sky.

For the first time, I felt more than satisfied.

I was free.

WHAT GOES AROUND COMES AROUND

Jacqueline Shi

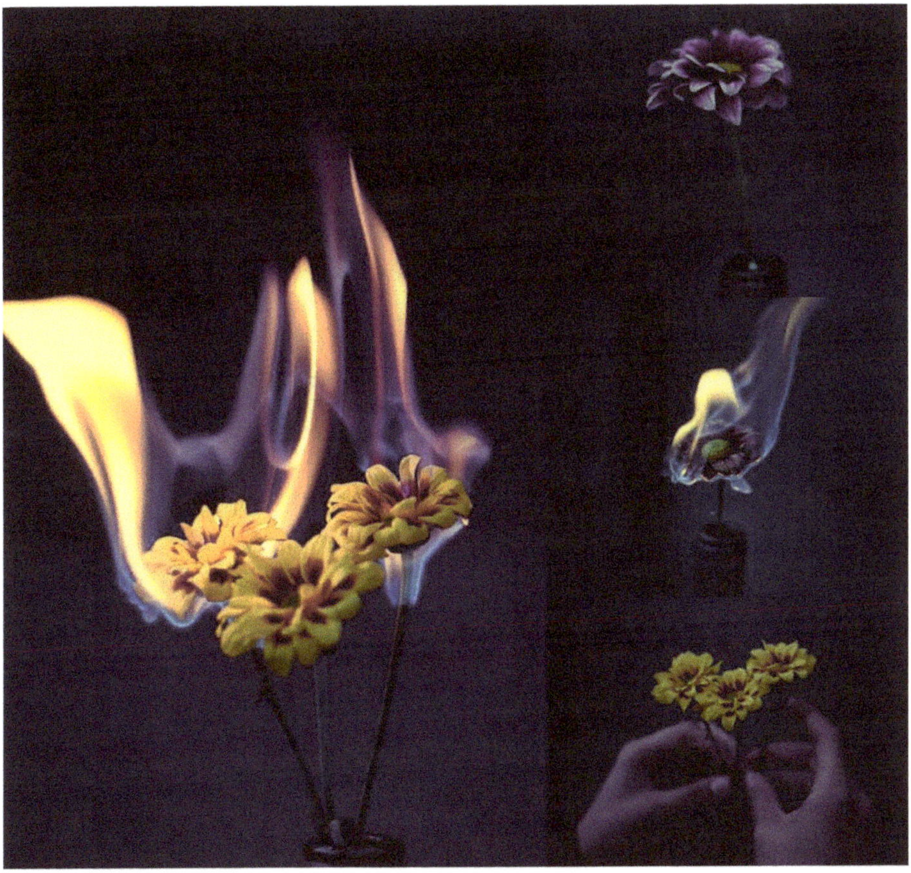

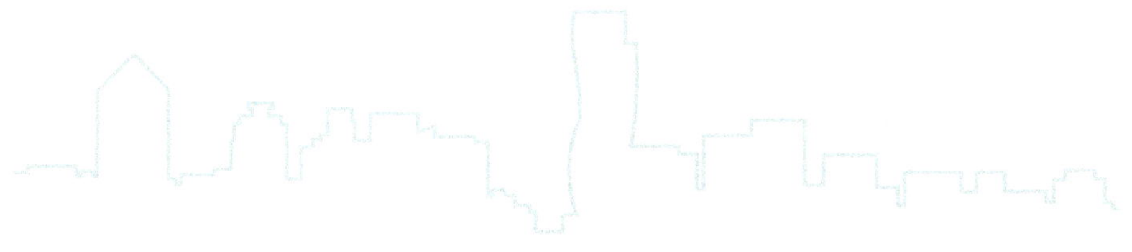

CHICKPEAS

Quratulain Dar

My mother once told me
That goats had to be fed carefully –
That all too often, upon finding a bucket of chickpeas,
They would gorge themselves, eating senselessly, eating, eating –
Until their insides burst.
We're quite a lot like goats, really.
Not for lack of intelligence –
Maybe the opposite,
Gorging ourselves, barely chewing our chickpeas
Before gulping them down, even though they
Scratch against our throats on the
way
down,
Barely breathing in between mouthfuls
Of handfuls
Taking up as much space as we can,
By the trough,
Batting away anyone who threatens our
'share'
We're not hungry. Are we?
Consuming in the hopes of filling some void
Left by absent fathers
Or mothers that squint at our stomachs
When they think we're not looking –
Hoping for a sign,
That this is it –
But no matter how far we dig into the trough,
There is none.
No epiphany, no blinding light
Shines through the chickpeas
No satisfaction, none of the 'happiness'
We promised ourselves
During the nights spent guarding our spots
But this is all we know –
So we dig.

PROTEGE A LOS ANIMALES

Sharon Low

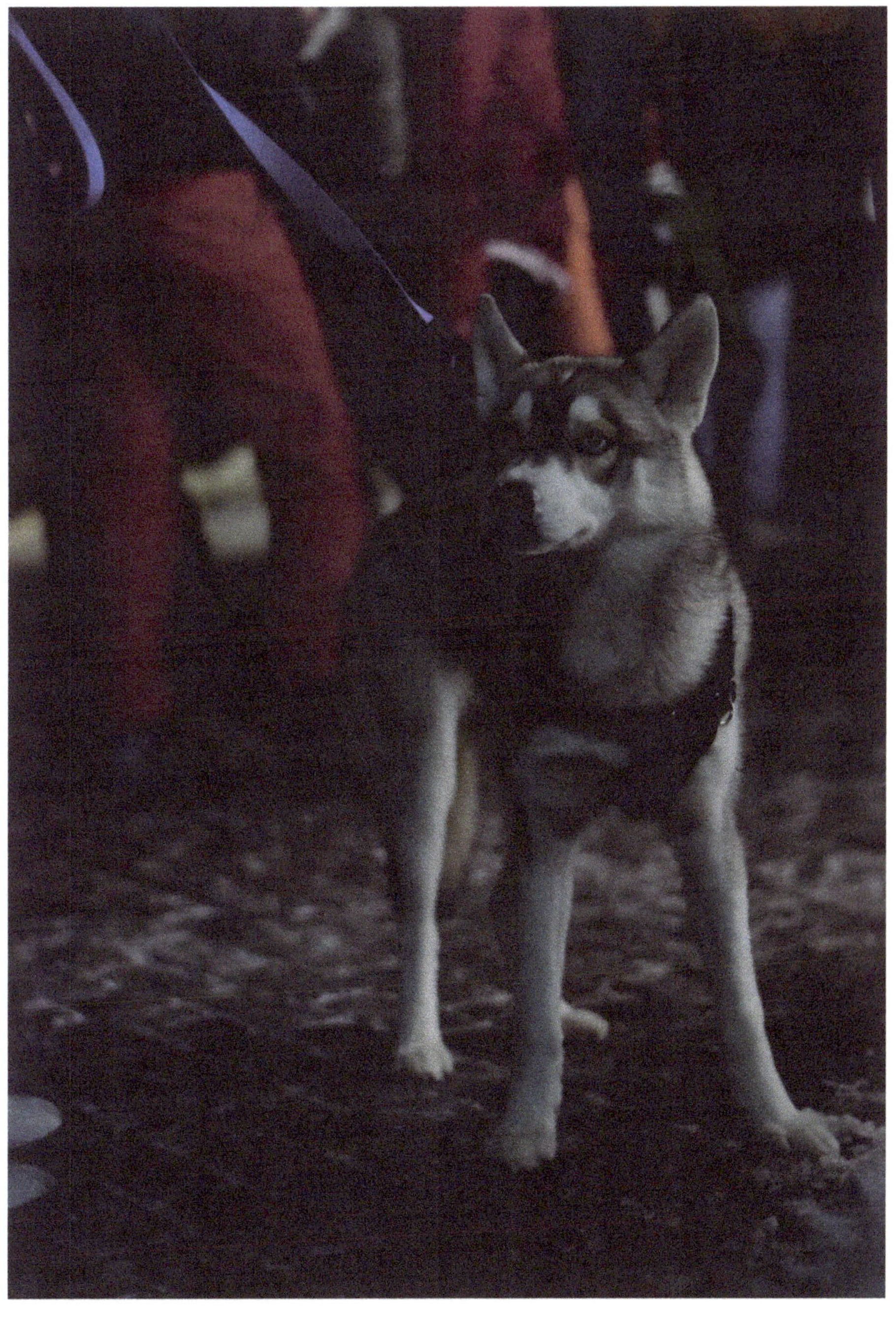

PAINT ME WITH YOUR COLOURS

Diya Jhuti

i love you
pink flows across my cheeks
red rushes through my veins
gold is woven into my hair
forever, i will love you

i love you
pink fades to white
red seeps into blue
gold melts into silver
forever, i will change for you

i love you
purple stains my cheek
blue stripes cut across my stomach
swirls of green branch out on my back
forever, i will be your canvas

i love you
indigo spots litter my skin
grey streaks entangle in my hair
black courses through my veins
forever, you will paint me

i love you
I am your painting
a sight on display for the world to gaze upon
people look, but no one sees

the marks that bind me
oh sweet caresses
how you fade
but remain etched on
my flat surface

i will never be blank
they told me to seek a life filled with colour
so i wait
patiently
while you paint me

you paint me with your colours
because you love me
strokes of fate
forever, I am your masterpiece

yes,
i love you

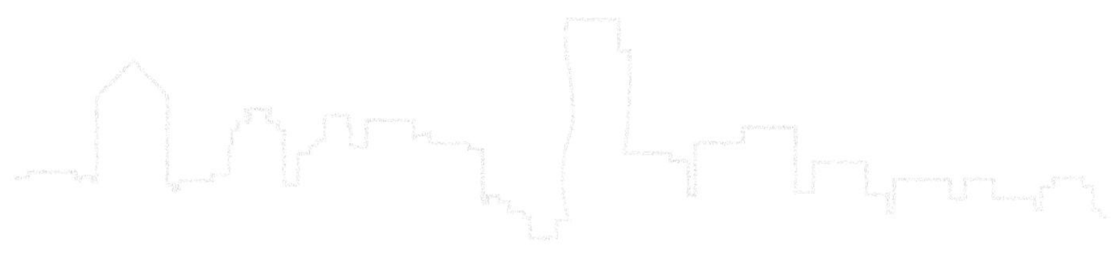

CELINA

Karim Machado-Aman

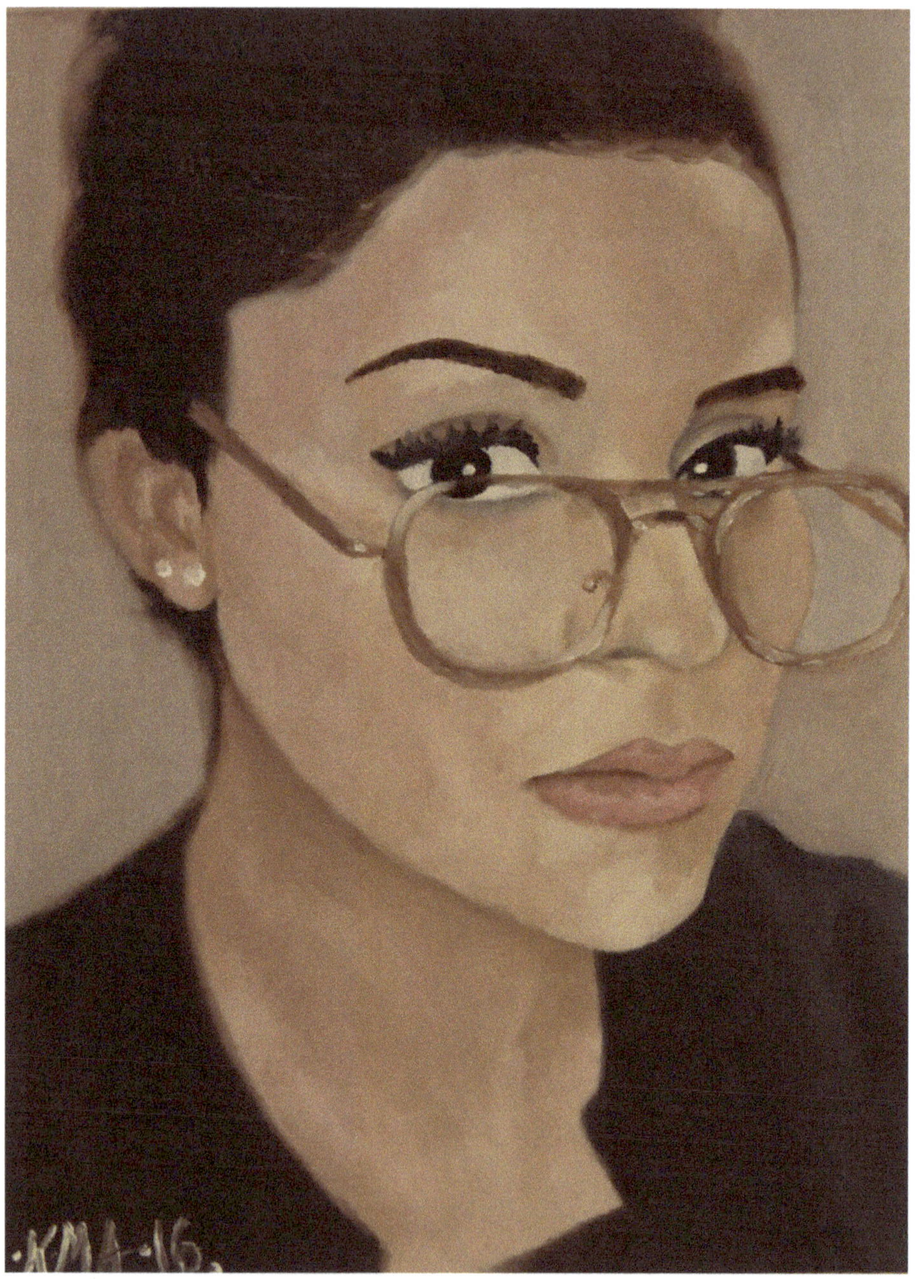

MARCEL

Karim Machado-Aman

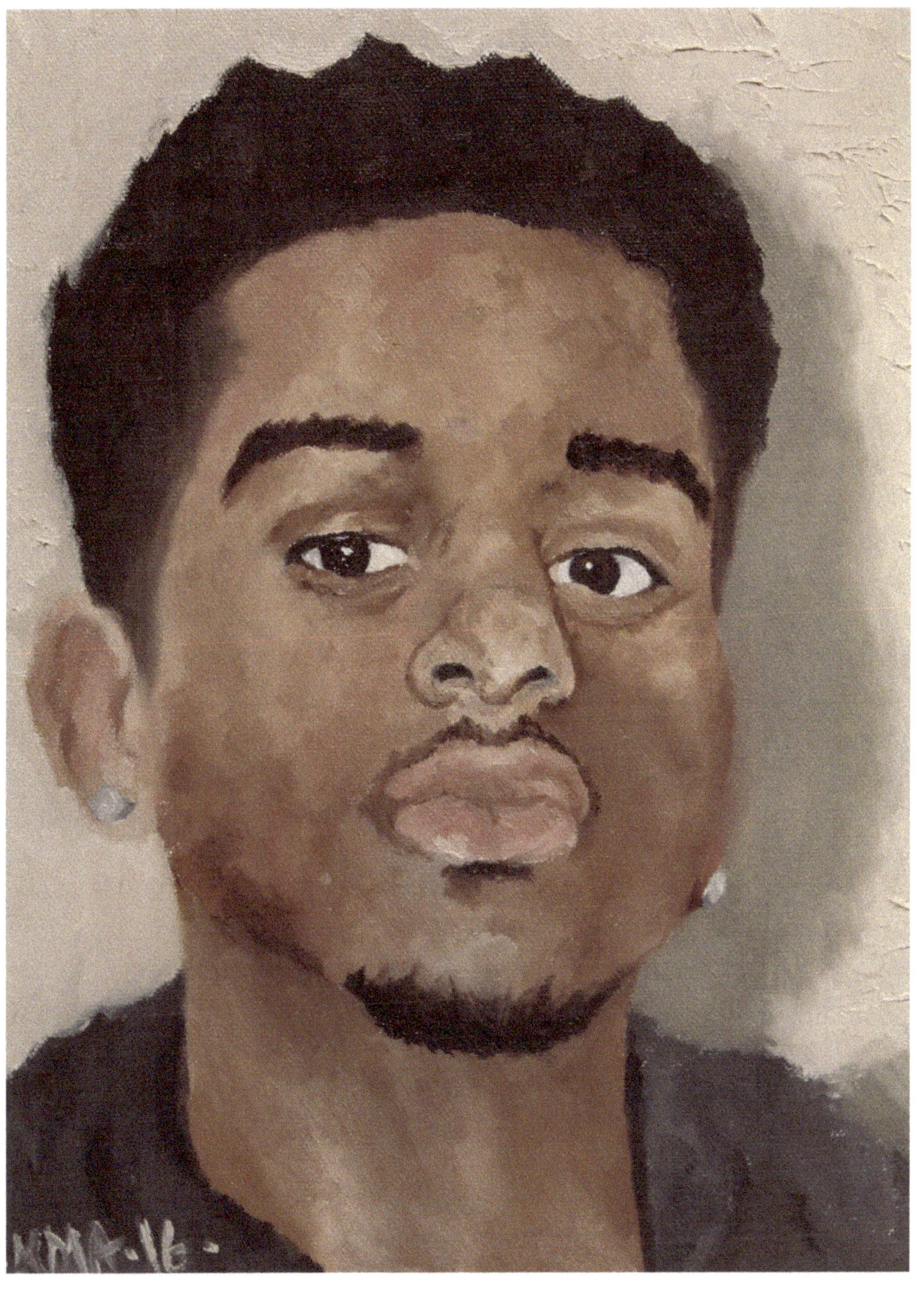

BITTERNESS

Shraddha Mishra

I've often felt anger towards the people who possess nothing but hatred for others – the people who constantly belittle and dehumanize those around them, solely because they are unable to love. As I've grown in my experiences in the last couple of years, I've realized that, although I seem to have every reason to be angry at the bitterness plaguing these people, I should be feeling sorry for them more than anything. Each time a friend messages me for comfort after being rejected by the person with whom they are infatuated or (perhaps) in love with, I fail to do anything but remind them to be thankful for their ability to love.

To be able to love someone and invest your heart and soul into them may result in a twisted sort of pain, but this ability is a gift. In the monotonous culture I find myself immersed in, I don't believe that enough people look at love and recognize it as a gift. In fact, they seem to be afraid of it. We run from it, because the potential heartbreak overpowers the sense of home and warmth found in another being. We cower in fear of it, because vulnerability is something that allows others to take advantage of us – our kindness and our willingness to serve them. And pain. Pain tears apart our insides and often disallows us from shedding light on *anything* within our minds, but I'm convinced that the paradoxical pain of emptiness and bitterness is fatal, too.

And gosh, is it difficult not to be bitter. There have been so many moments in which I've drowned in self-pity or been consumed by anger towards the actions of people around me. The more I experience these moments, the less love I feel for myself, for the people in my life, and for humanity. Ironically, these bouts of hatred ultimately result in a chaotic emptiness, in which I stop thinking about these moments at all and instead, allow them to bathe me in darkness. Although, on the other hand, it's difficult not to love, too. Whether this love is continuing to care for those who have hurt me or breathing to calm myself down before sharing the opinions which may hurt someone, this love continues to persist. Even when I've convinced myself to be bitter towards someone because they are undeserving of my presence, this love seeps through my skin and into my words and actions because as a human being, I am *made* to love. I feel sorry for the bitter ones not only because they feel alone but also because their identity as a human being is displaced.

It's simple to be angry at someone for being bitter, but it takes careful thought to recognize that this bitterness stems from the failure to love. It doesn't seep through their skin and into their words and actions. It doesn't gently remind them to be good to their loved ones. Its absence comes easy.

It's also simple to just let these people be. To allow them to drown in their bitterness. To back away when they lightly push.

If only we could help them isolate themselves into loving others, right?

JUAN FINGER

Fahad Bandali

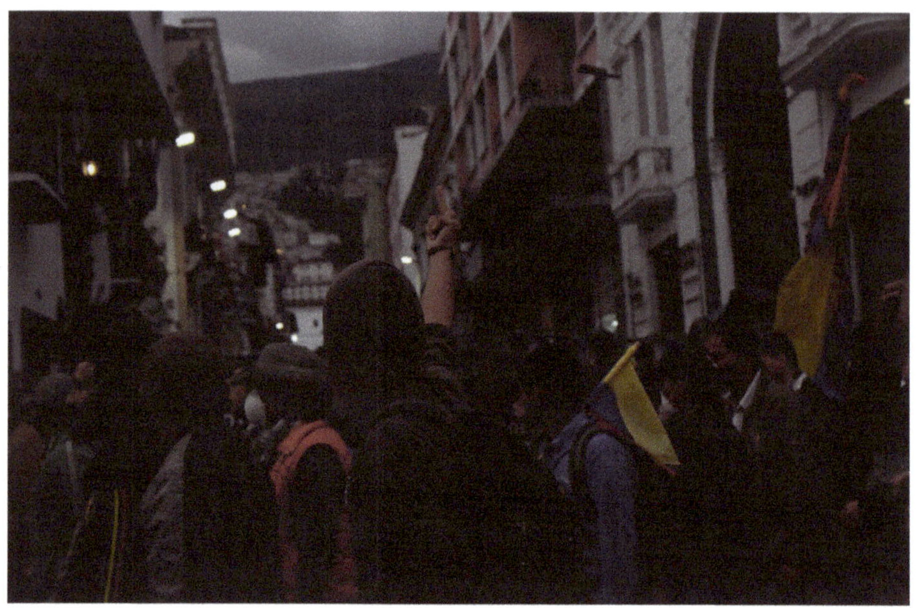

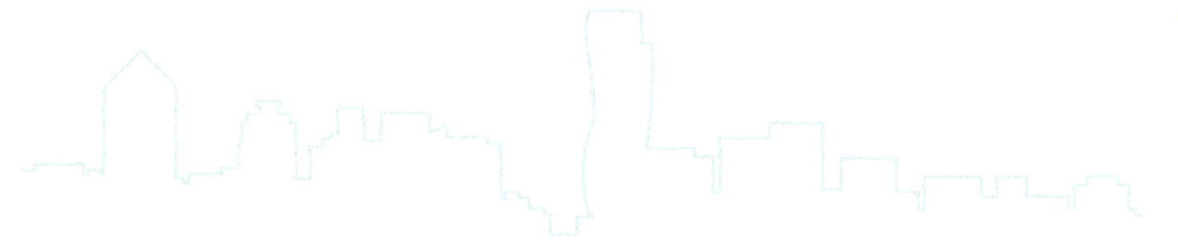

GRAPPLE

Carol Markos

At six years old I ask my mother why so many of the people at church have blue crosses on their wrists
I wonder if it's just the way their veins are
She tells me of a history long forgotten,
One where my people's language is slaughtered on the altar of their tongues
They used to make us wear crosses on our necks she said
so heavy our skin would turn blue
They called us blue boned
She says the blue crosses are just tattoos
I still think it has a lot more to do with our blood
Mama I have so many questions
Mama tell me why nobody here knows what Coptic means
Mama did you know that I'm a grapple
That while the apples share the cloak of my skin
The entire produce isle knows that I smell of grape
That I taste of question mark
Mama they ask me where I come from
I can only ever tell them where I am
I cannot help but realize that I feel like an immigrant on whatever ground my feet call home
In the third grade I convinced my best friend that I was Cleopatra's Cousin
That every morning I rode to school on a camel
I used to bring her resort pamphlets and tell her that I lived in those hotels
I am sixteen now and still feel like a tourist in my own country
They say Egypt is the kinda place you only go back to because your family lives there
Say it's too dusty
Too broken
Say you can feel desert on her skin
Valley in between her ribs

Say she is not enough
Anymore
Say Canada
Say free health care
Say your father and I brought you here so you could have a better life
Say people who actually follow the rules of traffic
Say "so exactly what are you"
Say both
See while Egypt raises goosebumps on my skin like pyramids
Canada waves her flag like arms saying welcome
When I cry, I weep with the Nile
When I smile, my eyes become the aurora borealis
Let my blood run through this ground
Let it tattoo the earth's flesh
Let me brand this holy body with my heavy cross
Let this be a reminder that
My bones will always be blue
My blood will always be red
My anthem will always be sung right in the middle of the produce aisle
But I am not singing alone
We are grapples
We are banoranges
And raspricots
We are avocangoappanandew melons
And we are home

SAUGA

Jessica Chiong

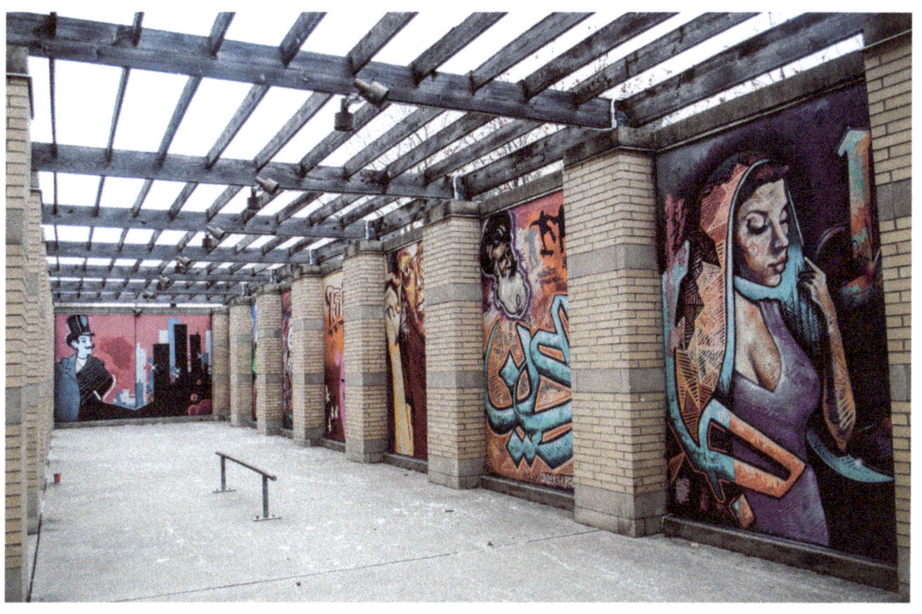

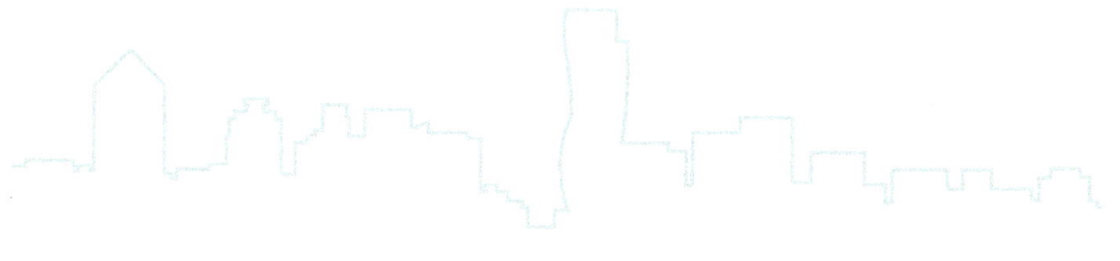

BEING "YOU"

Abirami Sudharshan

Never will I understand,
Society's affinity for the chameleon.
The idealization of uniformity.
The embodiment of an ever-present "need" to blend in.

I've come to witness,
Costume changes in multitude on the stage that is everyday life.
With every interaction
Demanding a varied demeanour – of pleasance, nonchalance or strife.

Quick and calculated are these spontaneous interchanges of personae.
Similar to one's selection of a coat,
In accordance with the conditions of the day.

Though I do see the practicality,
Of tailoring facades.
The resulting suppression of one's personality,
Transitions the experience from sweet to sour,
Much like an excessive gulp of lemonade.

Ultimately, it must be asked
For whom do you live?
Is this journey being made towards YOUR happiness?
Or is it for the satisfaction of strangers whom will of you, no second thought, give.

Your life is for YOU.
To enjoy, to laugh, to learn.
Be the person that makes YOU happy.
And you'll soon find
That everyone around you, will be happy too.

SCOTT MESCUDI

Karim Machado-Aman

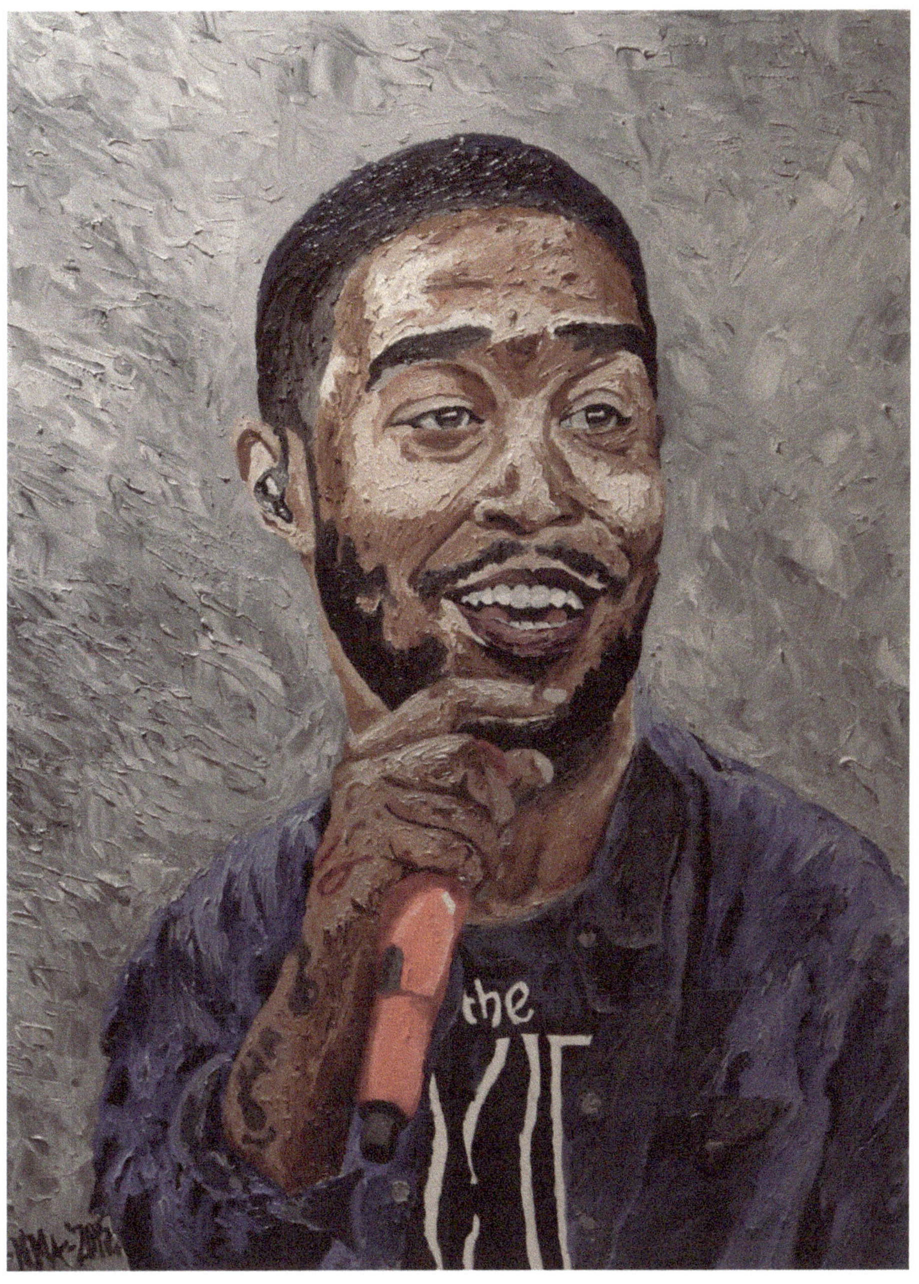

'AND FOR THE LADY?'

Maham Tariq

Marbled in a world thriving for perfection, tapping on the polished squares of hopes and erased imperfections we are yet to raise our hands in the name of god to pray, to love and to cry for those who have lost.

Lost in a world told to be perk and poised, a gentlemen's world is not to be destroyed. Placed in a one-way glass box, living in a misogynist joke, where my biological parts are the punchline and forced to live in remorse.

We shall live behind the words of Rosie, Steinmen and McClung, as we are equal and shall be one. Impressed in clay are buttons and knee-highs, pregnancy tests and silence, forced to be laid in a statue formed by man, it's time we see the time of dawn has passed.

The world around has forgone and seen much more than what is kept between, yet the facts of these acts are not justified, so its time these eyes see much more than one-way but to open to a spectrum of possibilities, and realize that virtue is kept in every disposition.

The rasp is now placed in a women's hand.

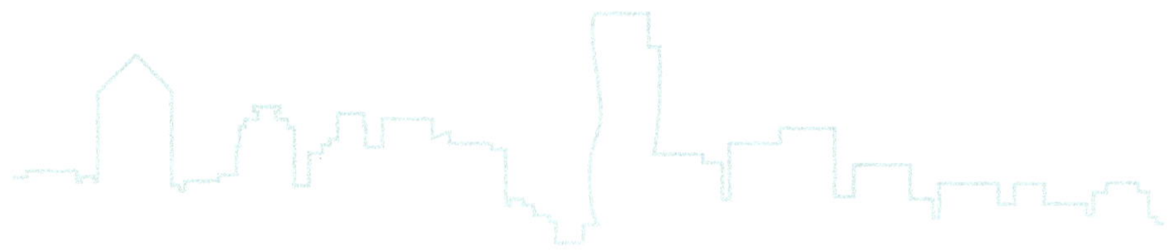

OUT FOR A WALK WITH MY NASTIES

Tahreem Alvi

On Saturday, January 21st, 2017, I marched amongst thousands of individuals ready for our voices to be heard. We marched alongside mothers and fathers, young children with their eyes wide, best friend with their arms linked and posters in hand. It was honestly such a surreal experience to be surrounded by so many people fighting together, supporting each other. I got chills every time the audience shouted "SHAME!" at the top of their lungs, smiled wide as we chanted, *"Look over there! Look over here! Feminists are everywhere!"* and was almost brought to tears when the organizers came out, eyes watering, talking about how a bunch of strangers came together to make this march happen and how incredibly wonderful this whole journey had been. Attending the women's march was truly an empowering experience that I am so extremely thankful for it and so, so happy that I was able to be a part of it. These photographs capture some moments of the march and every time I look at them the feelings I felt are brought right back and I relive the day once again.

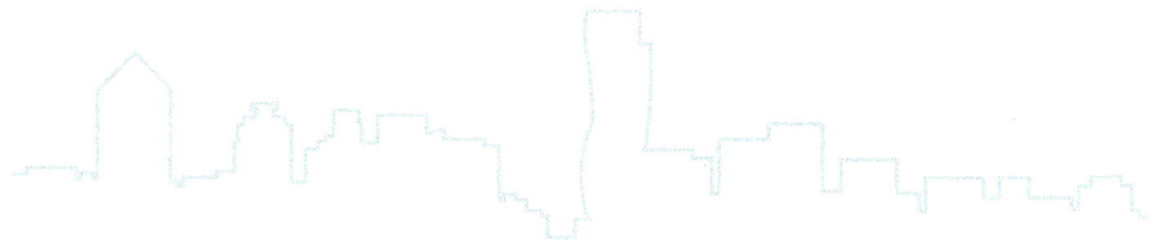

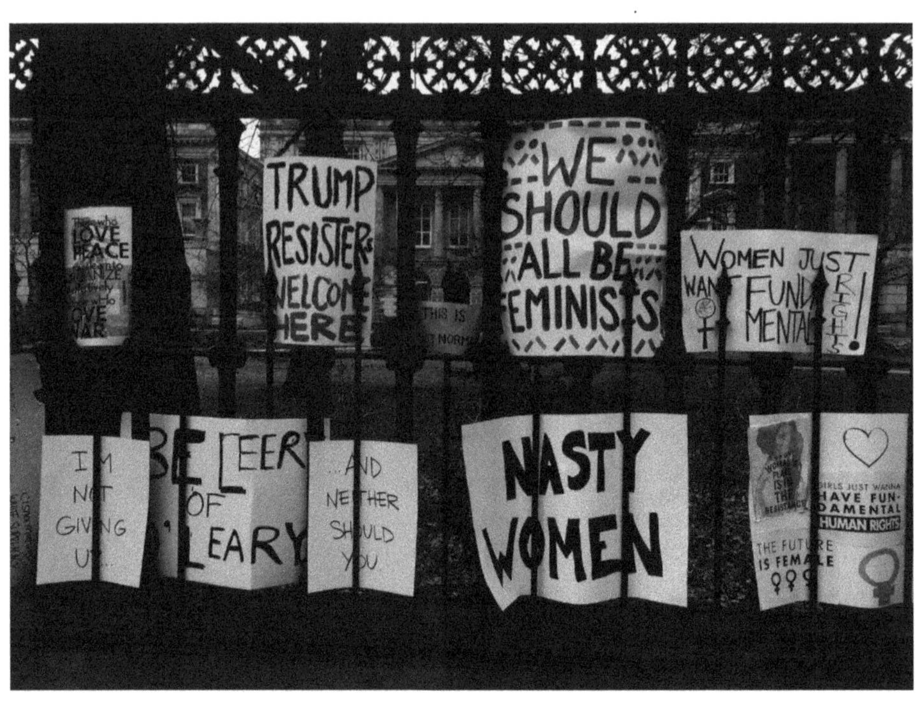
TRUMP
RESISTERS
WELCOME
HERE
WE SHOULD ALL BE FEMINISTS
WOMEN JUST
FUND
MENTA
RIGHTS!
I'M NOT GIVING UP...
BE LEERY OF O'LEARY
...AND NEITHER SHOULD YOU
NASTY WOMEN
GIRLS JUST WANNA HAVE FUN-DAMENTAL HUMAN RIGHTS
THE FUTURE IS FEMALE

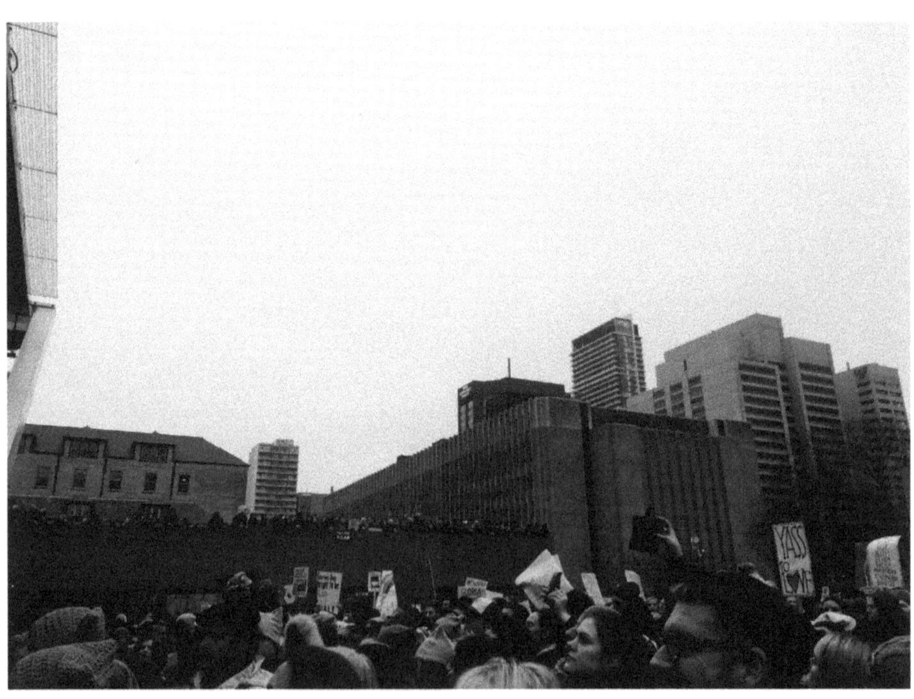

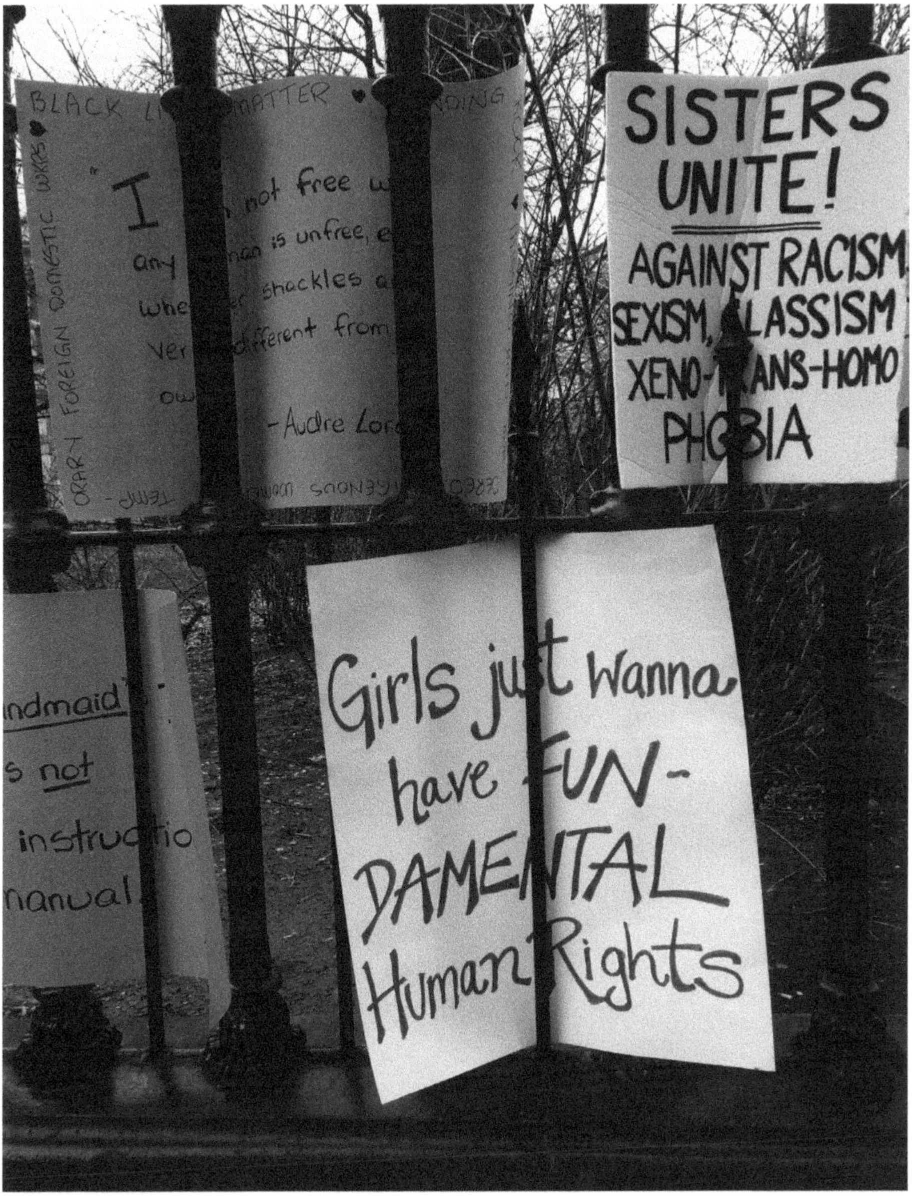

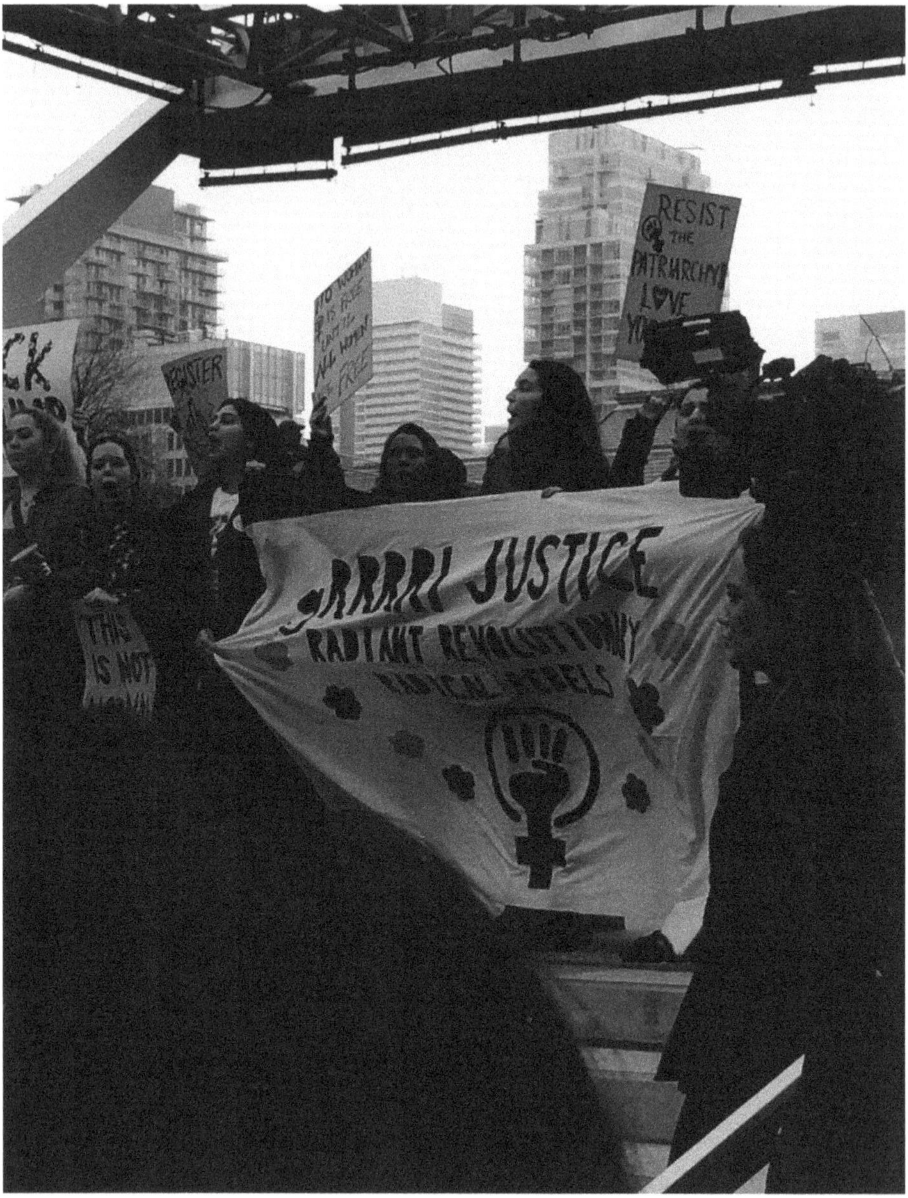

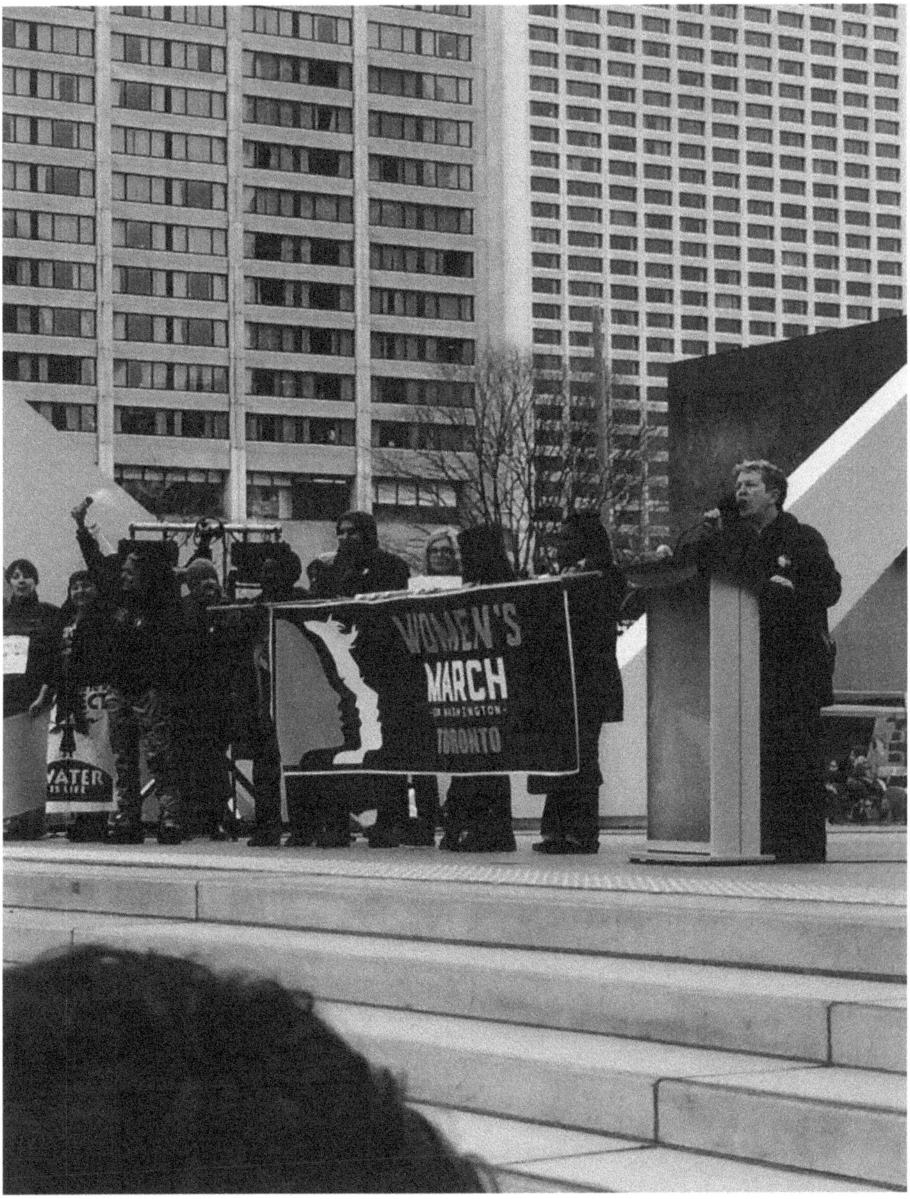

LOVE LOVE LOVE

Za

Love,
In the face of tyranny
Dip my blood stained knife into black ink
And write me a letter
Tell me the truth, where you want to be
In your dying days
Tell me what makes your clock tick,
Who your favourite director is
Sing me your favourite song over your blown-out speakers
With the bass turned up a little too high
Drunk laughing at me for lighting my cigarette backwards
Your tears stain my favourite sweaters
It's a little too much,
A little too late for this
Missed calls from my parents plague our pockets
Afraid to go home
We are more than death and taxes
Planning for a future we might not live to see
The taste of smudged bubblegum lipstick
Is stuck in my mouth
The stinging loss in your eyes reminds me of
Why people hold hands
Cigarette burns on my neck to distract from
The violets and the blues

Love,
When it hurts to be away

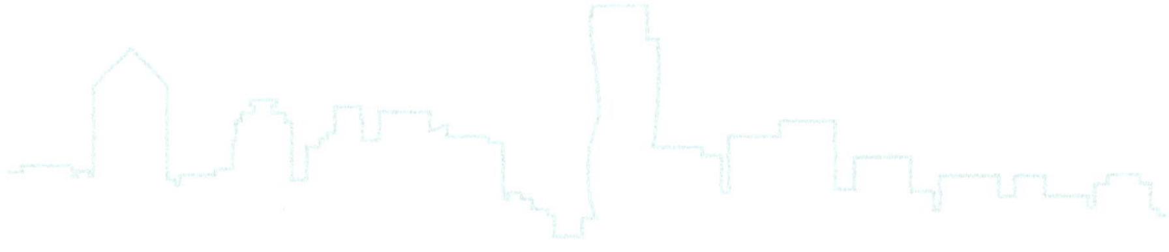

PHOENIX

Khyathi Rao

When you are bold and bright and full of life,
And reliving by the memories, all bittersweet,
And gently delve, and fantasize them as a treat
Your face is agleam, without any rife.

How many times have you gone into this stupor,
And reminded yourself about events black and white;
But one problem, stopped you from becoming a phoenix in flight,
And reminded you about being a primate.

And shaking yourself out of the trance,
Whisper, in a sweet tone, how your memories,
And youth define your otherwise lifeless bodies,
And start again from scratch, like a phoenix's stance.

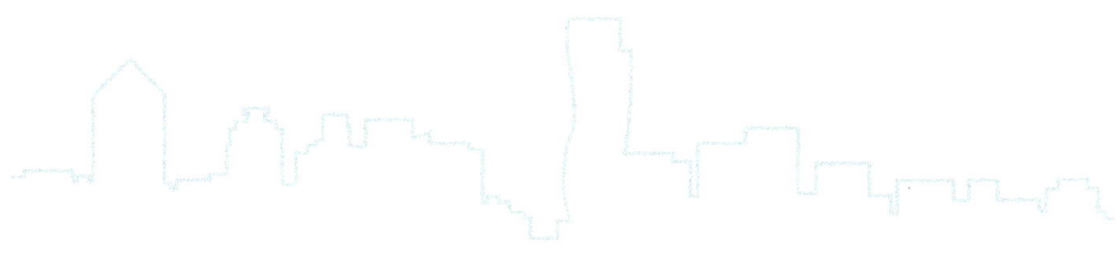

HAIR

Carol Markos

When we first met
I was 12
You
Were tall
Dark
And ready to make me handsome
Handsome
You liked to wrap yourself around me shamelessly
Fearless rebuttal to everything beautiful woman
Listen, I get it
Hairy bodies are a guy thing
Bear-like arm raised to carpeted chest in some sort of pledge of allegiance to masculinity
And you
You didn't really care did you?
Gave yourself free reign over whatever empty landscape of this body
Blanketed stomach
And arm
And thigh
Left no follicle unturned
Until I began to resemble what i assume early humans looked like
Not exactly ape per se
Just you know..
Definitely
Not
Beyoncé
I
Was not
Beyoncé
Now, as earth shattering as that revelation may seem it wasn't about to stop me so I began shaving myself into a new religion
I became familiar with its gods

Venus
Nair
Veet
And schick
Bowed my head to its holy trinity of
Soft
Smooth
And sexy
Familiarized myself with its rituals
Contorting my body in unsightly positions
Mirror in hand
Leg up on the bathroom counter
Every follicle was sin
Every wax strip
Every razor
Worship
One summer I dared look at my bikini like high school dropout to master's degree
Spent so much time shaving in the shower you could have used all of the clean water to sustain an entire village
Instead
Each drop like a flower petal fallen on the grave of my self esteem
I'm not saying that body hair removal is evil and that all women who do it are just blindly giving in to some cultural beauty ideal
I'm just suggesting that we ask ourselves why
Why does every hair on my stomach have to be a picket sign in protest of the patriarchy?
Why is it that when he grows out his facial hair he can say it's because he isn't feeling a shave right now
But I can't wear shorts on hairy legs without being asked about what kind of political statement I'm trying to make
Or maybe you'll just assume I'm lazy
Or gross
It took me too long to realize that my body is not a smooth canvas or blank page
It is abstract pop up novel encyclopedia dictionary
It cannot be defined
It is that through which I define

I have decided that my life is too precious to spend severing the parts of me that will always grow back
I am covered in stories and colours
And this
Is just hair
It's just
hair

TRANQUIL MORNINGS

Warren Wong

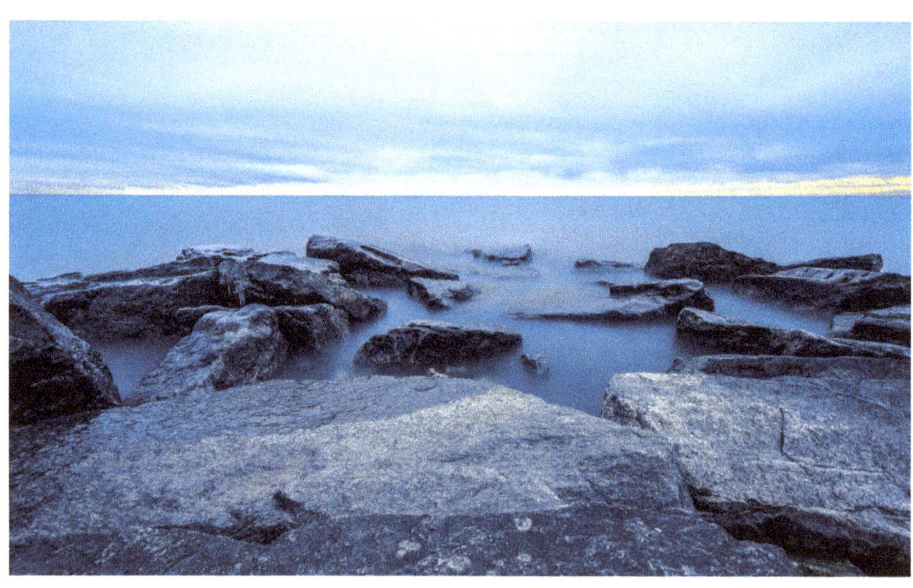

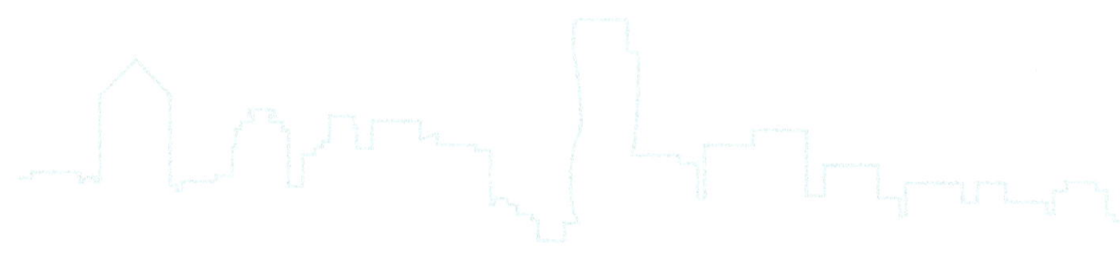

YOU HAVE YOUR DAD'S EYES

Aiken Yong

People always said, I had the eyes of father
But one day when I fell off my bike, as my eyes teared up I saw my resemblance with mom....

Mom progressively became more like a mime
She grew more silent
And her face was always covered with makeup
So she didn't have to makeup anymore stories

See dad's best friend was Jack...Daniels
Jack gets abused a lot too
Jack wants mom to know what he goes through
Jack wasn't a good influence to dad
His advice on the road was bad
Now dad's gone cause of Jack
But that probably made dad like Jack more.

People always said I had the eyes of father
But I don't want to ever be like him
So remind me
Even if I wanted to
I wouldn't be able to
Follow in his footsteps
Cause he covered up his tracks when he left me

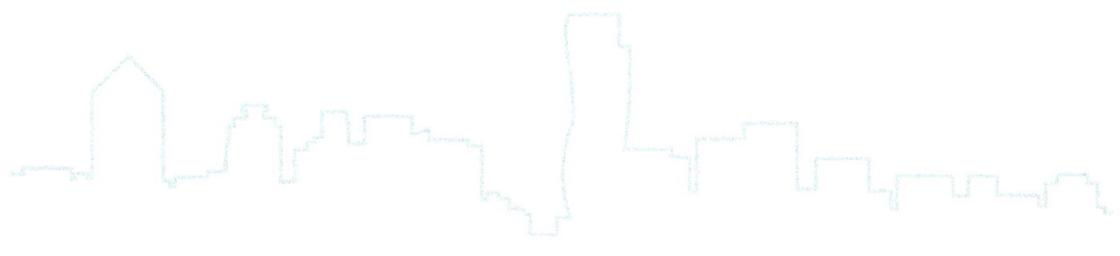

VIEWS

Ani Srikanth

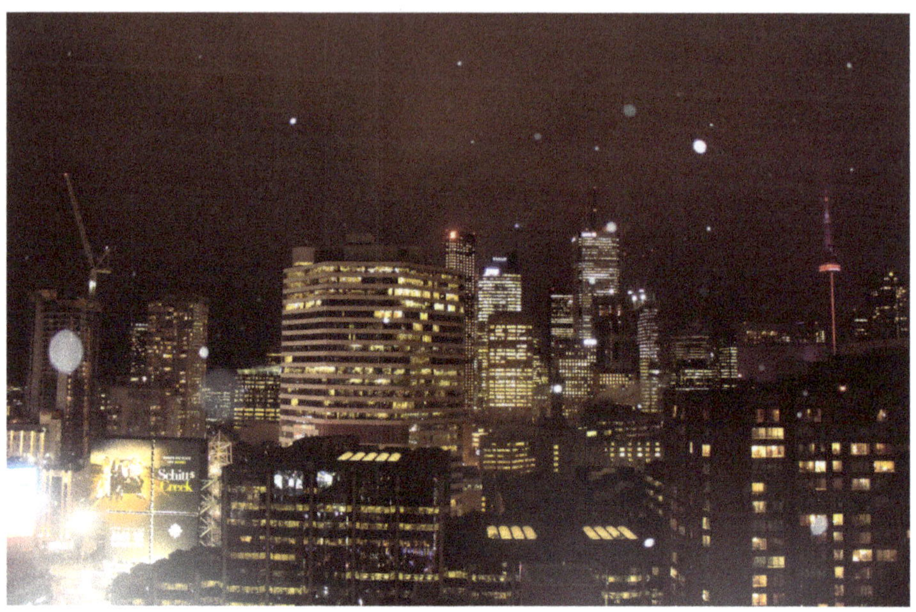

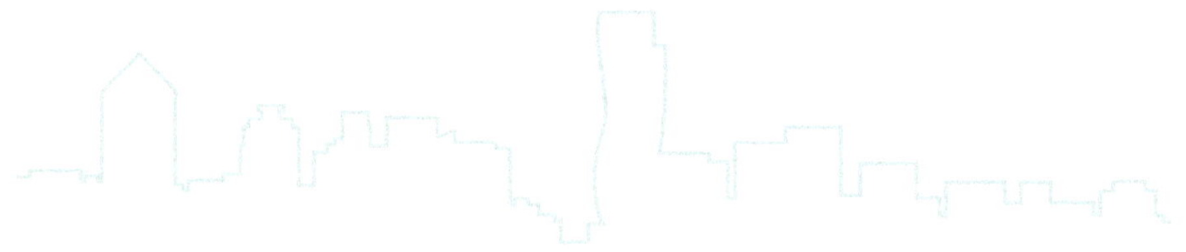

VIEW OF THE 6IX

William Lam

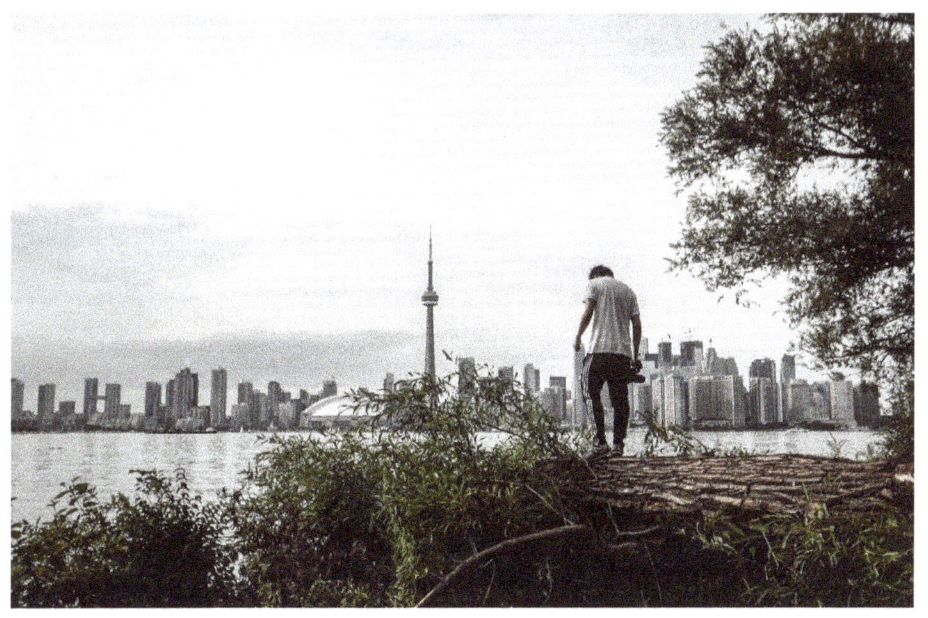

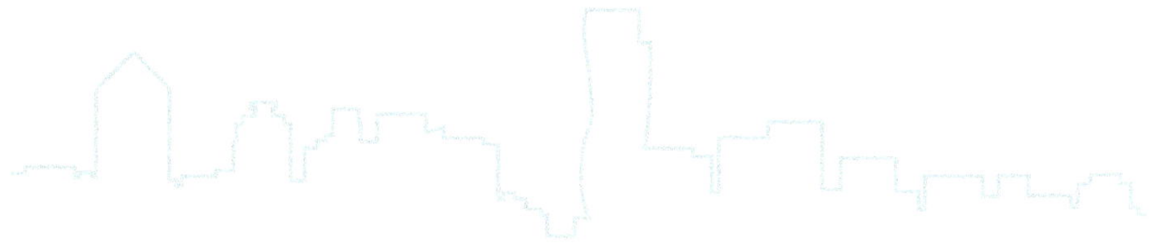

A BLESSING INDEED

Khyathi Rao

Beggars lining up along crowded streets, outside worship places and even at the railway station, is a normal scene in India. Hence, passers-by pay no attention to one, when they come to them, asking for money to buy food for their children or themselves. You can see their frail bodies walking around, persistently hoping for a kind soul to make their day. It is a pitiful sight, but not much can be done. Or that's what I thought, until I met a small girl with her mother, begging outside the temple, one day.

As we were exiting the premises, they came to us and asked for money. My grandfather gave them hundred rupees, and they bowed at us, with gratitude in their eyes. As they turned away, and walked, my grandfather turned to me and said, "It is not always that you are born into a privileged family, that takes care of you and wishes the best for you. Therefore, it is very important that you always be thankful for what you have and help those in need. It is not their fault they are in such a situation. Remember, even how little you give to them, they will be very happy, and gratefully remember you in their heart always." Instead of replying, I stared at the girl and her mother. What surprised me is that they did not spend the money for food or water, but rather books. They bought a few books from the bookstore across, and the girl started reading them out loud to a group of kids, sitting on a mud field. It was unclear, broken English, but just the actions and the sound of her voice made the children laugh. After finishing one book, they discussed what had happened in the story.

Curious about why the girl would spend money on books, rather than important needs, I asked her mother, and she said in a proud voice, "My daughter you see, she has a selfless soul. She spends a little money on food and water. Instead, in hopes of becoming a teacher for people like us one day, she tries to teach the younger kids, with what little she knows." She stared at her daughter again, tears welling up in her eyes.

As I walked back home with my grandfather that day, I realized that it does not take much to lead change. Today, my grandfather gave her hundred rupees and with which she produced joy and happiness worth a lot more, with small smiles on the little faces. I do not know whether she will remember me, but I will never forget her small, determined face in my life, ever, because she taught me how to come across various odds in life, and achieve my dream, nevertheless.

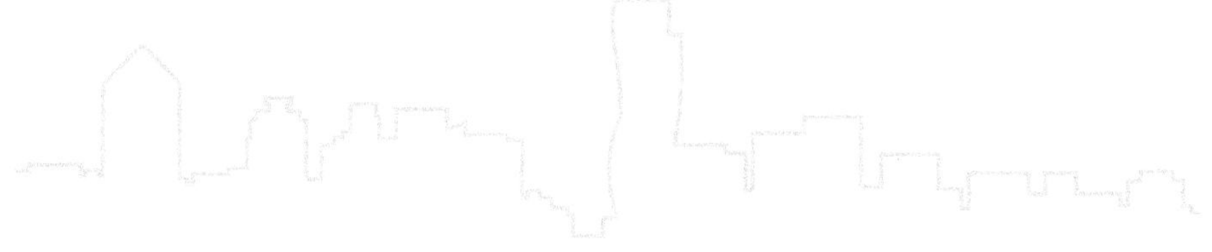

MY HANDS

Diya Jhuti

My hands caress the world
with soft gentle strokes
loving hands,
radiating hope

My hands are the soil
to bear the fruit of life
birthing a safe haven
to plant the seeds of inspiration

My hands are a bed of warmth
to hold perfect struggles
enveloping a spark of innovation
moulding endless possibilities

My hands are a catalyst of motivation
shaping a plethora of passion
sifting through vast expanses
of knowledge

My hands add a dash of dedication,
a pinch of peace,
a cup of confidence,
an ounce of opportunity

My hands were made
to create
to challenge
to change

My hands
Give.

TODAY A READER, TOMORROW A LEADER

William Lam

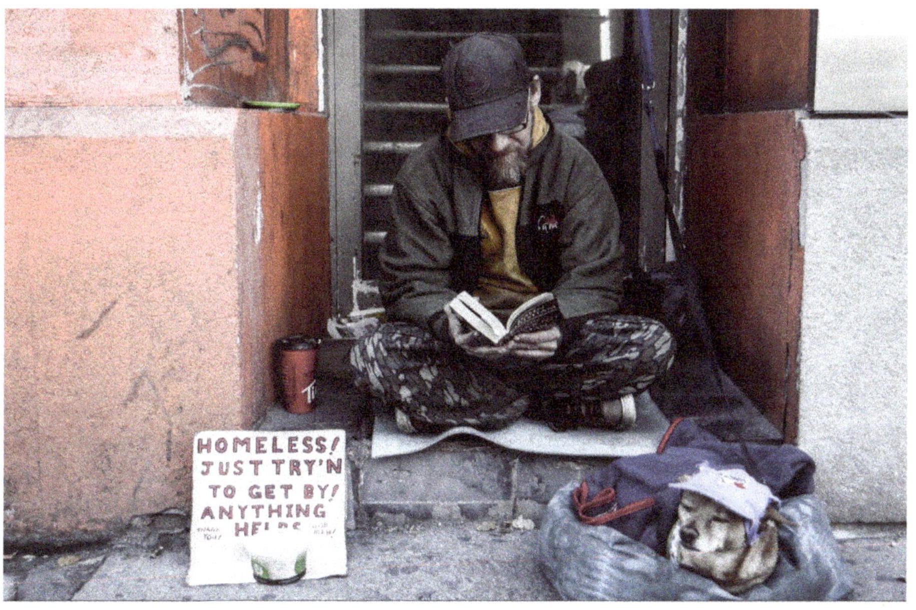

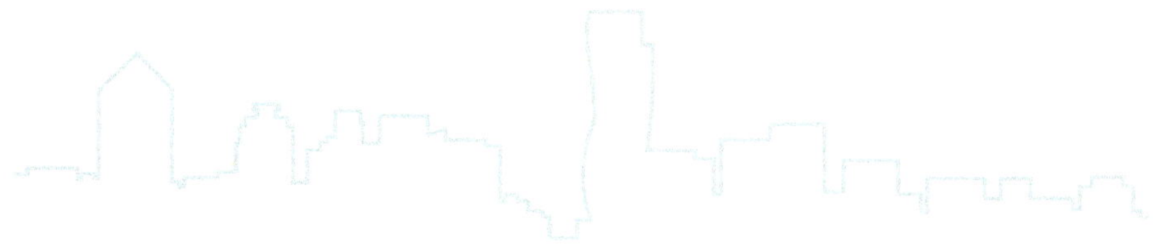

HIPS

Shraddha Mishra

Wider hips.
Wider hips and longer hair.
Wider hips, longer hair, and the ability to bear children:
These are the things that make me a woman.

Among broken people, wretched freaks, and mundane behaviours
The only thing I am is a tasteless flavour

Days, months, years, and centuries
Have been wasted by you, telling me I'm mindless,
Faceless,
Less.

My only purpose as a person is to be an object
Who knew having more of one hormone meant being a living
defect?

A universal declaration of rights?
Subtract the universal and subtract the rights.
And if you want full marks, add domestic abuse.
Multiply that by 4 *million*.
Does it seem like a few?

What we have left is a fragment of paper,
One declared by a half-empty species,
Who've been cornered and chained.
Portrayed as an empty shell of skin and bone,
It seems a portion of this world sits at the foot of a throne.

And me? I've been thrown in.
I've been thrown into a box signed 'Fragile: handle with care.'
My value is relevant if my face is fair,
I'm a human being, but only in prayer.

'Adam comes before Eve'?,
It turns out, we can't even breathe.

For you, the skin on Malala's ear was torn.
For you, my freedom is forever scorned.
And this box? It shelters me.
It seems I'll never truly be free.

My knuckles have been shoving at the stale cardboard,
Yet here you are, refusing to walk down this road.

Tell me one more time that I'm overreacting.
Tell me one more time that my dreams aren't being held captive.
Tell me one more time that men are here for me to please.

Because apparently,
That's where my worth ends, anyway.

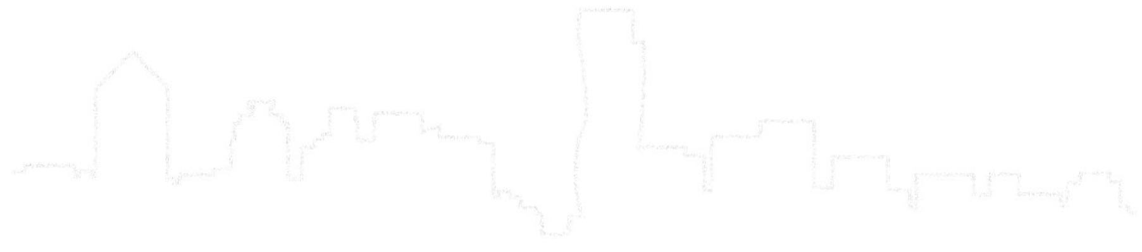

BREAK OF DAWN

Daphne Nguyen

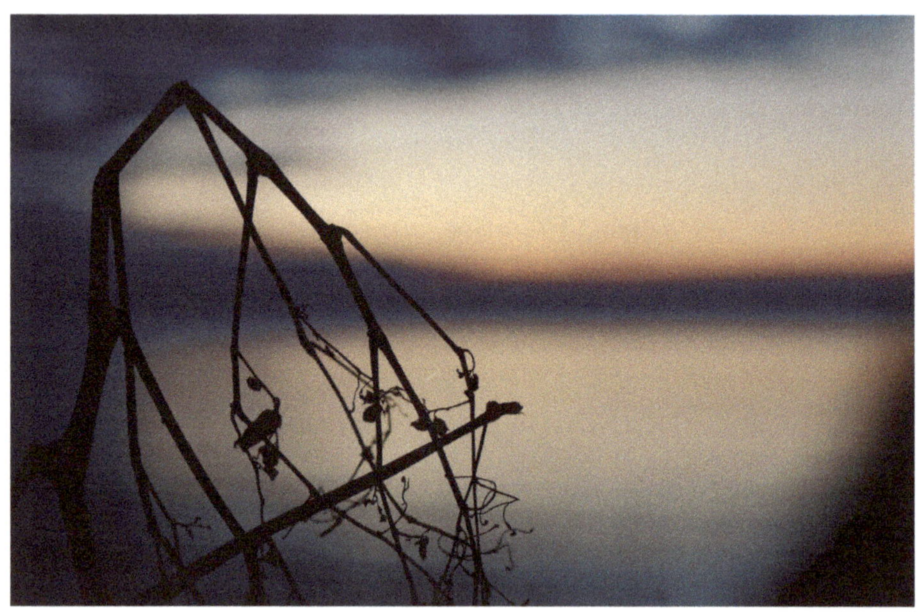

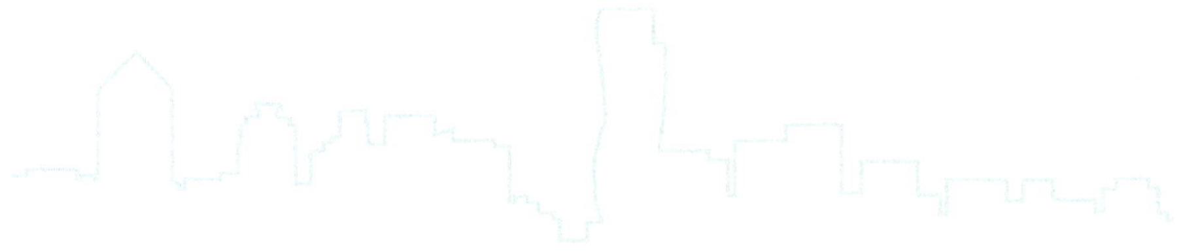

WHEN SHE WAS NINE

Anonymous

When she was nine, she was told about beauty.
She was told about women with slim figures,
And models who could not be any bigger
Than she already was.
When she was nine, she was told that she was too fat,
That "look, your thighs should not be much bigger than that,"
That if her stomach was not flat,
Who would want to love that?
When she was nine, she had not known that she would start
Hating the body that she called her own,
That in just a couple years she would be repulsed
By the taste of food until she could start seeing her own bone.
Just at the age of eleven she was weighing at ninety-seven pounds
Until she lost it all in less than a month,
Until she saw the number on the scale,
But that number still could not satisfy her struggle to be smaller.
When she looked in the mirror she knew why she skipped dinner
And questioned how she was not getting any thinner,
Even though she could not remember the last time she really felt
full.
Her rolls were still there and her thighs were still as big as ever
And her waist did not seem to grow smaller
And she was two more than nine
Hoping that she would never be a size nine.
When she was nine, she dreamed of looking like a girl in a fairy tale,
In a pastel dream.
With a tall yet petite stature,
With long hair flowing down her back,
With the glow of beauty and grace emitting from her body.
She could not see that girl when she looked at herself,
And instead found flaws which found their way to form
Self-deprecation.
But slowly she began to realize,

That she should not be the one to cry,
That she should not be the one to hide her body,
That she should try to love every little part of her
That was exactly five feet and one-and-a-half inches high.
And although she has extra chub around her,
Hey, she can't help it—it's her sexiness overflowing.
Big thighs don't cause her grief anymore but smiles,
Knowing that they make her just like Beyoncé, just alike.
She is a big girl now
Quite happy in her own world,
Knowing how much better it is to be happy with
The extra skin around her bone.
The anguished feelings sometimes rush back to her,
Feeling like they may never go away,
But they always do.
Always.
So if she could turn around and talk to the little girl
When the little girl was nine,
She would tell her about real beauty,
The kind that comes from how big you smile
Or how loud you laugh
Or how you make everyone's hearts around you happy.
She would tell the little girl to love every little thing about her,
Tell her that beauty isn't something that others can create for you
Because beauty is something you create for yourself.
But she would never tell the little girl that she is not pretty enough,
That she does not compare to the others
Who are trying their best to be their own kind of beautiful,
Because that is something a little girl should never be told
Especially when
She was only nine years old.

WE ARE ONE

Jacqueline Shi

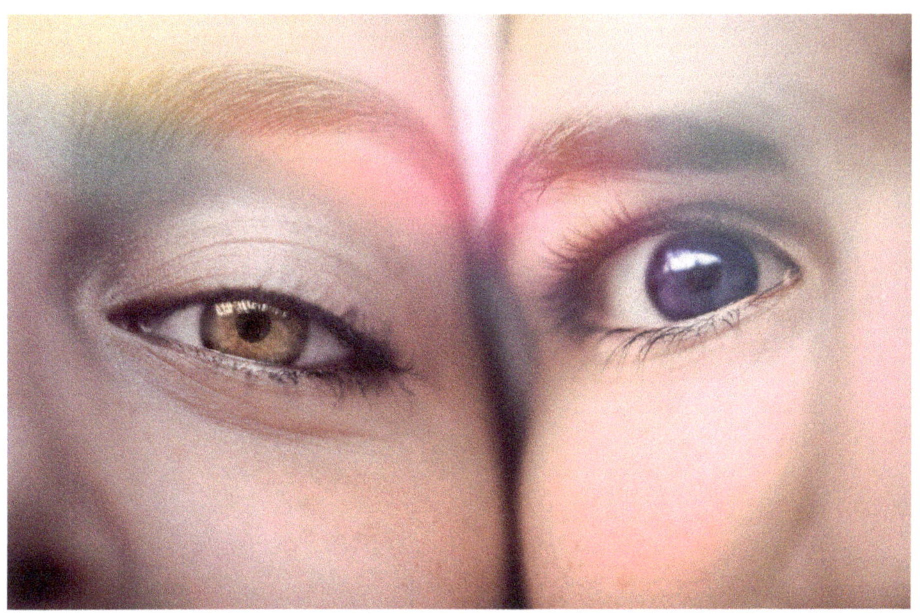

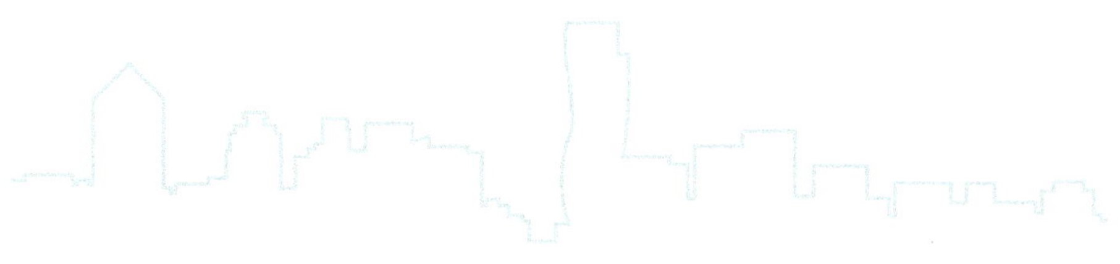

A PROMENADE ON EVOLUTION ST.

Prasiddha Parthasarathy

"We are all in the same boat in a stormy sea, and we owe each other a terrible loyalty." G. K. Chesterton

In my evolutionary biology course this semester,
We learned of our origins from the Last Universal Common Ancestor.
To me, beyond a doubt, this was a supreme revelation.
If we go back far enough in time, every albatross, iguana, and *E. coli* arose from the same, primitive creation.

Of course, over evolutionary time, we have diverged,
Forks in the tree of life to get to where we are today.
Natural selection and genetic drift have worked tireless shifts,
Ultimately to favour and procure more intelligent creations – humans, we say.

Sometimes it's easy to get lost in that thought –
I mean, what were our odds of beholding this manifestation?
Had just a tiny, indiscriminate detail worked out differently in our history,
We could have easily been mongooses, newts or some kind of crustacean!

The genetic odds of us making it this far, into the most "intelligent" creations of being
Are so indescribably small, a magnificently miniscule number.
And so, I think what Chesterton meant was that in this finite, human life,
We owe it to our fellow humans, to sustain ourselves and one another.

See, the astute creatures we are, I don't think we're oblivious to good reason.

We know what we are doing wrong –
That gut feeling when we throw away food, that's our conscience, my friend.
That feeling in the pits of our stomachs when we see a homeless person on the street, that's our consciousness, my friend.
That feeling in the backs of our minds when we think about sorting our trash into recycling and composting, that's our conscientiousness, my friend.
It's time to stop snoozing those alarms.

In today's world, we've heard it more than enough:
The rich grow richer, the poor yet poorer.
But of late, the gap has spawned into a chasm with no signs of reprieve in sight.
It's time – we need to empower each other, all of us, set the books right.

It's one thing when evolution causes inevitable change,
But if people were to be wiped out because of oversight and neglect, it would be an utter shame.
See, the "poor" and the "rich" are mere distinctions we've made.
Frankly, each human is our closest family, and of aiding them we should not be afraid.

It would be a fallacy to think that our actions don't impact the future.
There must be a reason evolution brought us this far!
We owe it to ourselves, and each other, to make our community last.
We've done too much taking, and it's time to give back to nature's reservoir.

All in all, it is our choice how we impact our travel on Evolution St.
So, together, let us set off on the right path, to accomplish mankind's greatest feat!

EPHEMERAL NATURE

Sereen Aziz

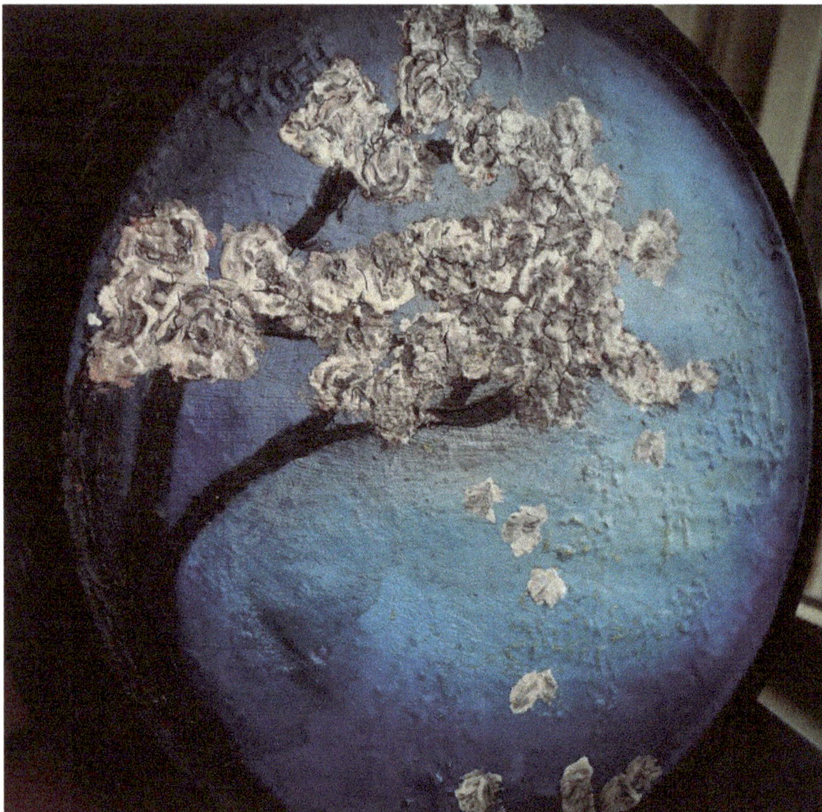

FORESTS

Surutiga Ranjan

A tall glass building
Stood in the middle of a forest
A proud creation
Of a CEO
Who gloated about
And cared about opinions
So asked every person
What they thought of his creation
And every person
Told him it was fine
Until one day
The oddest thing happened
He asked the same question
To a lady walking by
Who walked three dogs
And wore a necklace of flowers
She spoke honest words,
And told him what she thought
His pride was broken
And confusion filled his mind
So he questioned the lady
And asked her "Why?"
And all she said
As she left to walk through the forest
Which was filled with the lives
Of many plants and animals
Was
"Look at it, in another perspective."
And the man's eyes
Followed the women into the forest
And he saw the luscious green trees
Surrounding his building
And how he had ruined
The beautiful image
Which was once whole.

REGIONAL RAIL IN THE GTA

Adrian Aliu

This map depicts a future regional rail network for the GTA that I planned. Regional rail is like rapid transit that operates on existing freight and passenger rail corridors, with frequent service and electric trains. It essentially creates a regional rapid transit system without the cost of tunneling or building tracks. I made this map last year, and if I were to change it, I would add more stations near downtown (Liberty Village, East Harbour, Gerrard Square). I have been really into maps since a young age and since I started reading them I noticed that there are so many gaps in the local transportation network, so naturally I began creating maps that show the solutions to these problems. Lately I've really been focusing on making them aesthetically appealing, so they take a really long time to make.

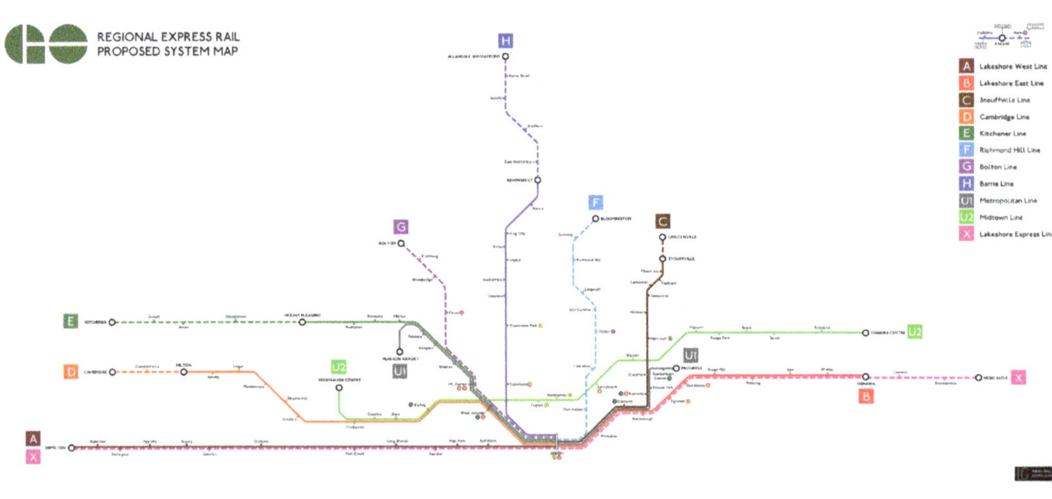

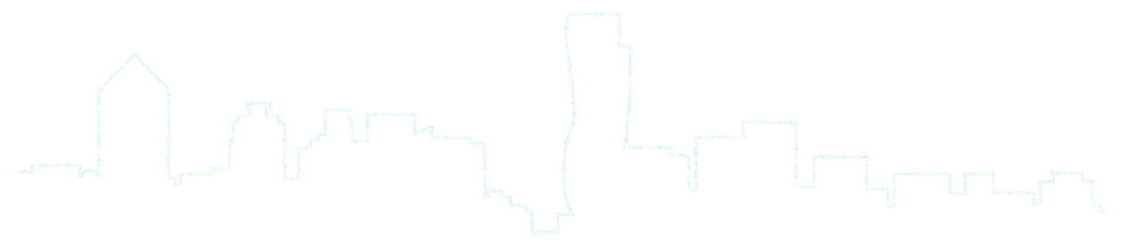

AMD

Ave Mariabell

Hello, my name is Ave, a small-town Aussie girl who moved to Toronto three years ago. Moving here has helped me reconnect with my passion for living a creative life, and I was inspired to share my art with the world through Ave Mariabell Designs (AMD). AMD is a series of ultra modern, minimalist, city skyline designs which aim to unite people together by celebrating cities that we love. With AMD, people can take a piece of the city they love home, whether it is a large-scale wall decal or small gift item. Instagrammers have fallen in love with the minimalist look of the skylines, and many want it in their homes to showcase cities they have travelled to. I aim to inspire people to share the journey of celebrating cities we love by encouraging custom requests from the community. This is the most unique selling point, as it allows me to engage with locals and their ideas, making each design have a feeling of exclusivity to each customer.

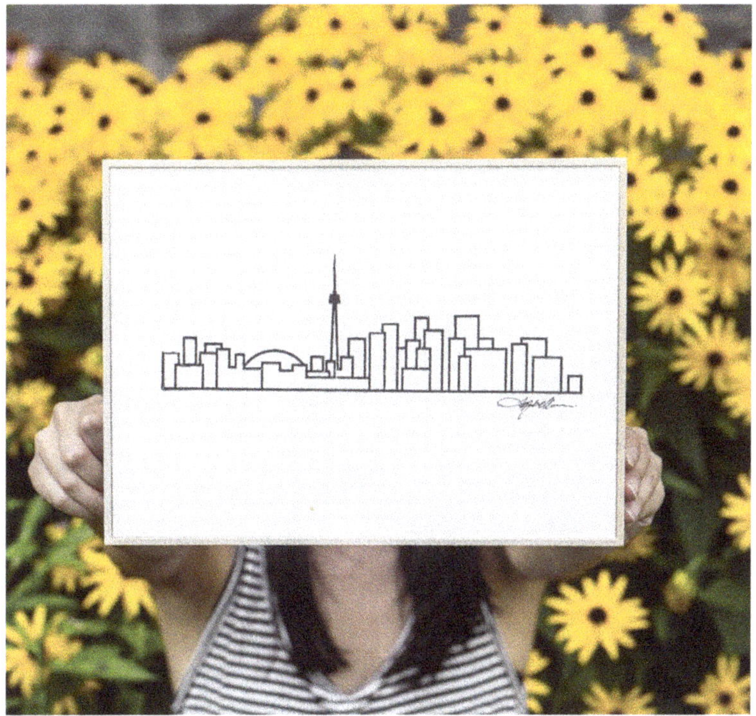

DRIFTWOOD AMBITIONS

Jordan Currie

Legacies evaporate
despite how much I wish they wouldn't.
The carvings we've made into earth's corpse
erode and fracture some time or another.
She swallows us mercilessly whole
and by twilight's yawn
or sunrise's rouse
or any time in which we are breathing
we are gone
taken into her everlasting grip of
apprehension.
She's selfish, but nonetheless
so are we.
Like mother
like children.

I said I'd wanted to change the world.
(how original.)
Get in line kid,
don't we all?

I dreamt of sailing on
driftwood ambitions,
conquering the injustices of the world
battling the systems which drown the oppressed,
let me be an amplifier for unheard cries
and fight for the luxuries known as equity
but our tidewrack crowds the shore line
and I am no hero.
Not a saviour, nor
a memory in the making.
Merely a small piece of driftwood
trying to make her mark in some capacity

before being swept away by the ever-rolling tide.

On the plethora of restless nights when
sleep won't come,
I think of what put me here,
in this body, this skin,
this community,
this privilege.
I don't think anything did
yet accidents happen.

No, I wasn't granted the answers
to the universe's inquiries
but yes,
for some reason a power in the sky cannot assemble,
I was given me.
I wrote this.
These words, these sentences I've strung.
They are mine.
Mine
however fleeting they may be.

Calling all donators,
calling all healers
and protestors,
fighters and warriors,
veterans who've picked themselves up for the thousandth time
and new youth learning the ropes.
Calling all volunteers,
the rebuilders of debris
and refillers of empty soup bowls.

Calling to you,
painter of hope,
songwriter of glory,
dancer of pain,
poet of truth.

Compose the symphony to make sense of it all,
tell the story with the movement in your bones.

I was not destined to save the world,
rid it of its injustices and poverties
but perhaps my short time here
and my art crafted out of temporariness
can provide Something,
some small source of inspiration
to pass the baton along into oblivion.
This tiny,
temporary legacy.

GLOBAL WARMING APPROACHING

Anthony Moss

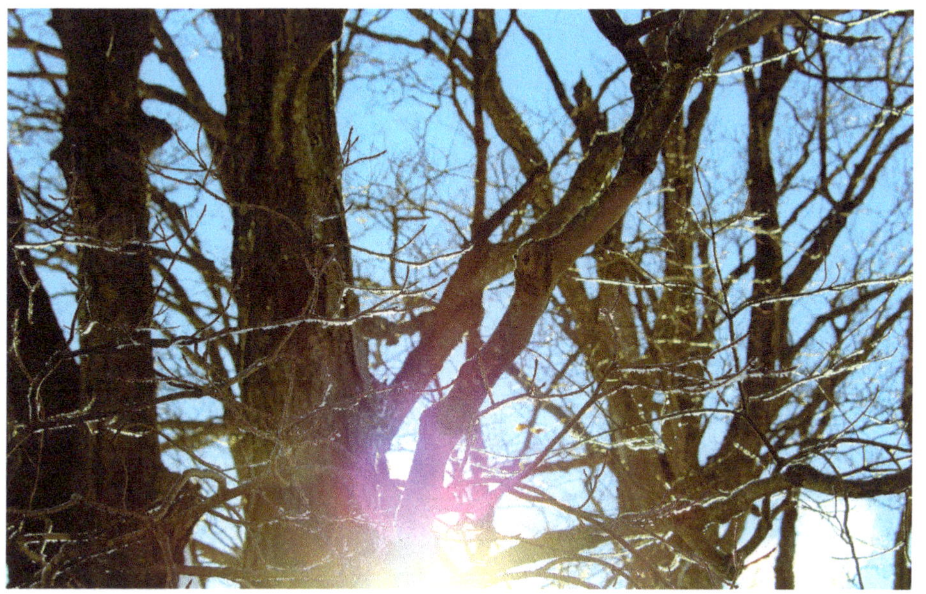

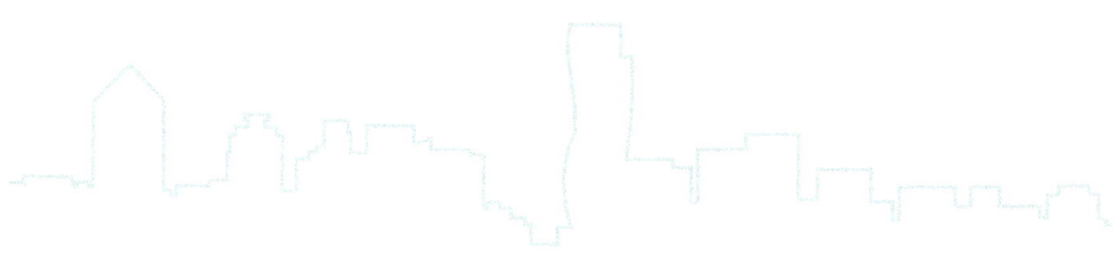

KINTSUGI

Sonya Zhang

Kintsugi is the Japanese art of repairing broken pottery with
lacquer dusted or mixed with powdered gold
(kintsugi: the idea that after we are broken and shattered *we
will still deserve to be put back together*)

Learning to love
All the worn out parts
(and all the shattered pieces)

It is my parents, coming to Canada 20 years ago
With a total of 30 years of education between them
(2 university degrees that meant less than 水饺 without 醋)

Fighting to squish their
stinky tofu
and
bamboo chopsticks
into a harsh Canadian mould that spit
up and chewed out anything
that wasn't as white as Wayne Gretzky
(and maple syrup)

Trying to figure out which one was Subway the sandwich shop
(and which one was Subway the actual fucking subway)

Trying to fit together a baby daughter and a life worth living
(with broken English)

It is knowing that every time they fell the only thing they had to fall
back onto was themselves

Kinstugi is when things fall apart
(and when things come back together)

It is finding the gold in broken English
(and 粽子 that will never taste the same)
(and a daughter with a
mother(tongue)
that will always be
for (eign)
to her)

Kintsugi is telling ourselves that no matter what we will always deserve to be put together

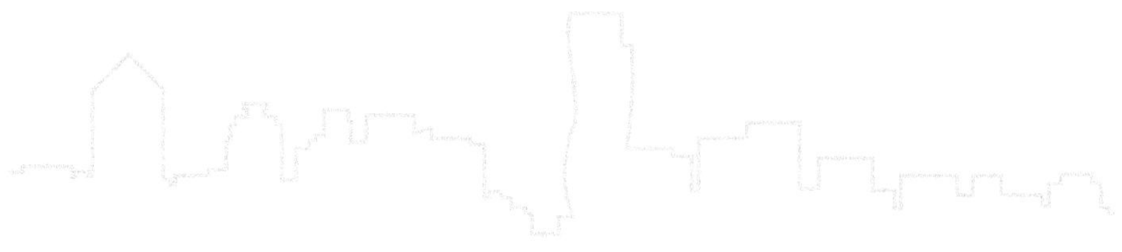

COLD WINTER

William Lam

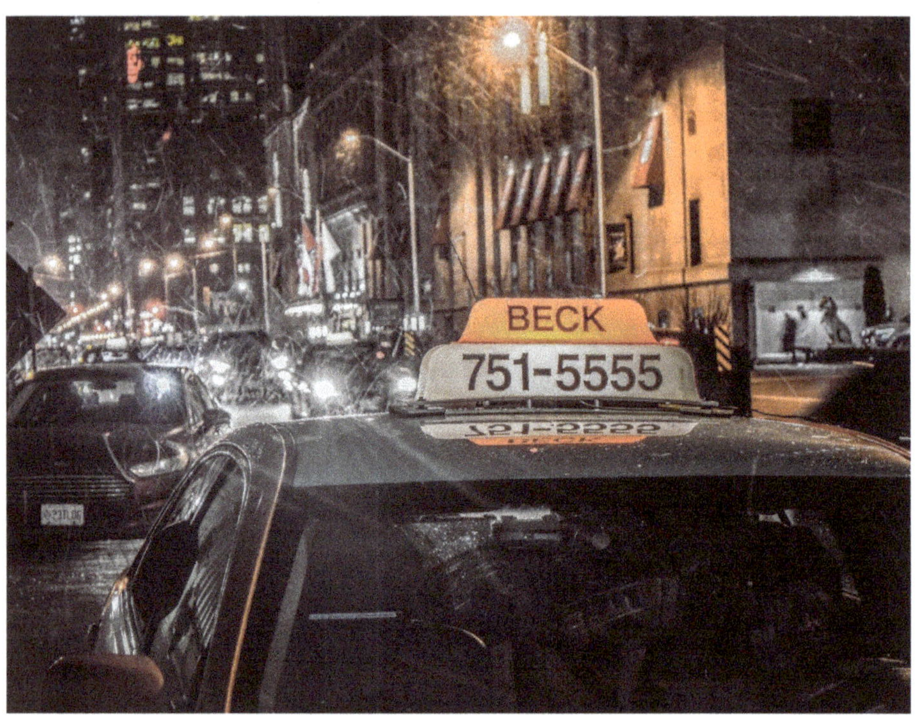

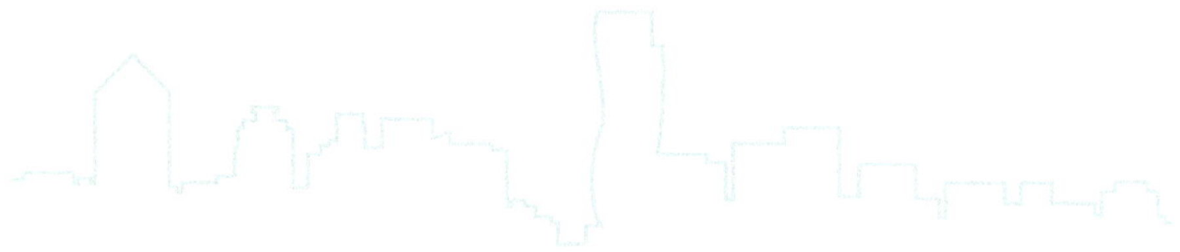

WHO WANTS TO TAKE THE TTC?

William Lam

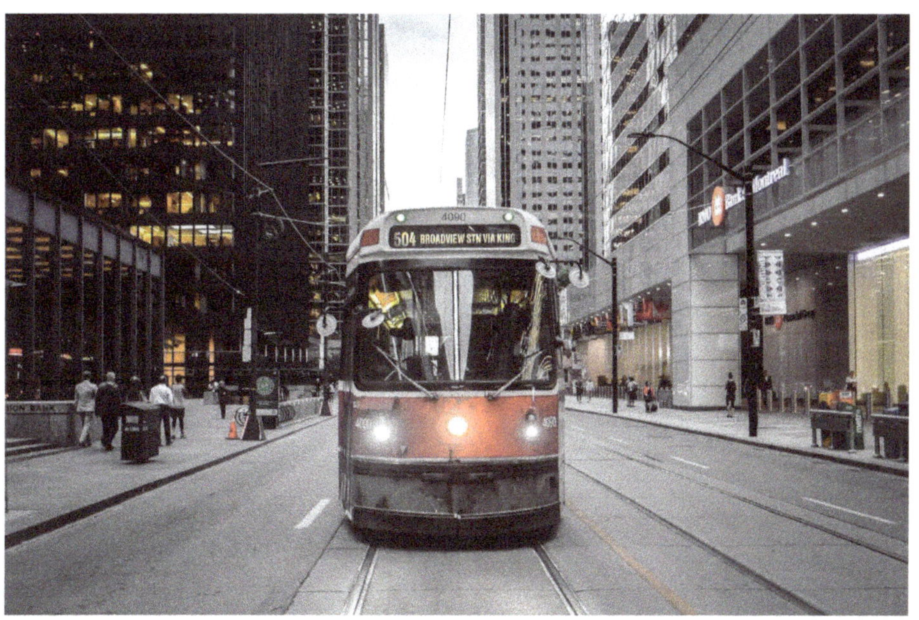

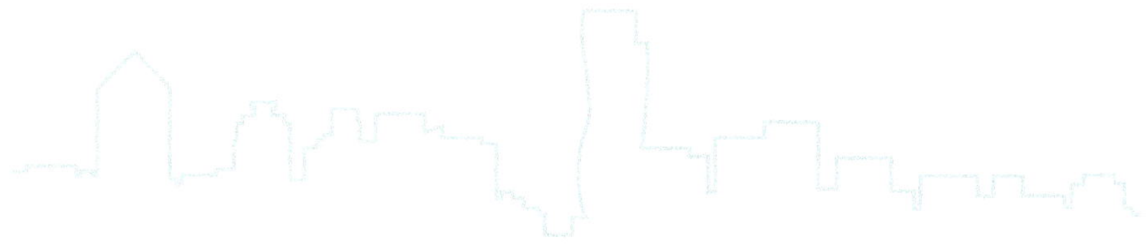

A CRASH COURSE IN LIVING

Za

you deny yourself the simple pleasures of the colourful; saturate the world you live in and seek shelter only in the hues of the mess we made

the same browns from the earth on which you walk are embedded into your skin

remember crash courses in living; stargazing on the hood of my brother's car

you were never big on small talk, you said that even broken hearts shatter into sparkling stardust

you'd rather turn the TV off and run your fingers through the static on the screen

only ever come down from an upward curve find contemporaries in temporary purgatory

only see the world through a prescribed rose tint take so much from the world and only give back in a pine box

there's no use in avoiding trips, they only make the fall shorter you write of your hopes and dreams from rock bottom

there's exotic dirt under those fingernails even Icarus' daring eyes did see the sun before they met death

darling love your irregularities, as even the most yellow of dandelions are not guaranteed even petals

love the shade of blush in your cheeks and the dark shades in your rain soaked hair love your name and the scarcity of keychains that belong to it

love your scary thoughts as they belong to nobody else but you, for every profound artwork belongs to a tortured artist

there is no force greater than the one cultivating amidst your skin and your bones

there's no use in denying yourself the simple pleasures of the colourful

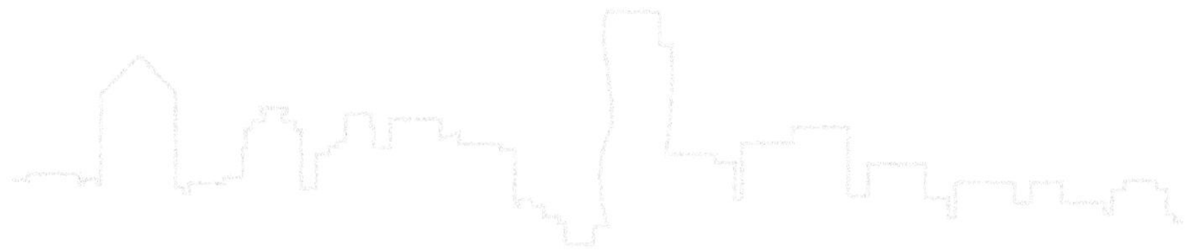

9:05

Moaaz Waheed

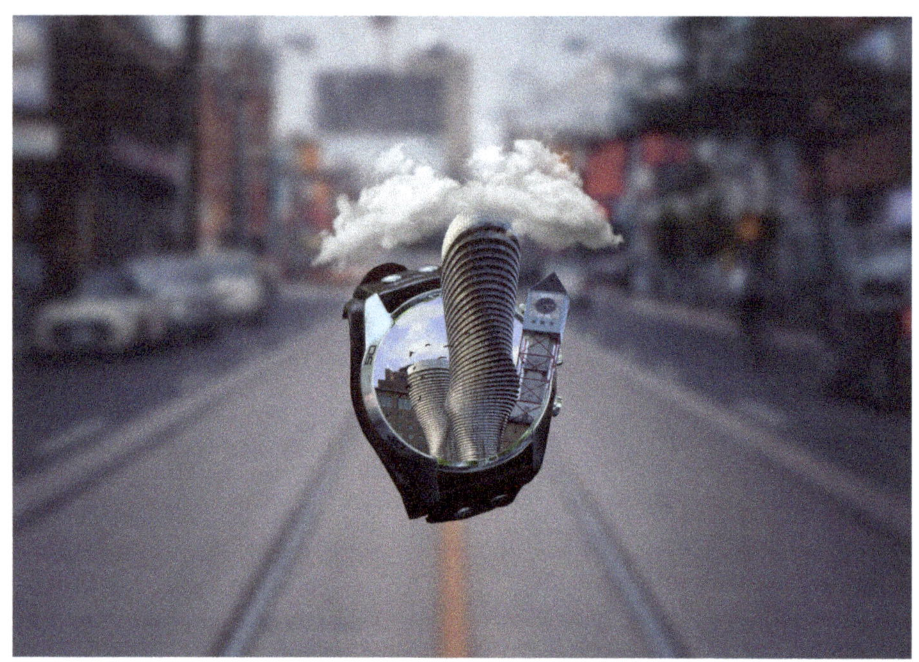

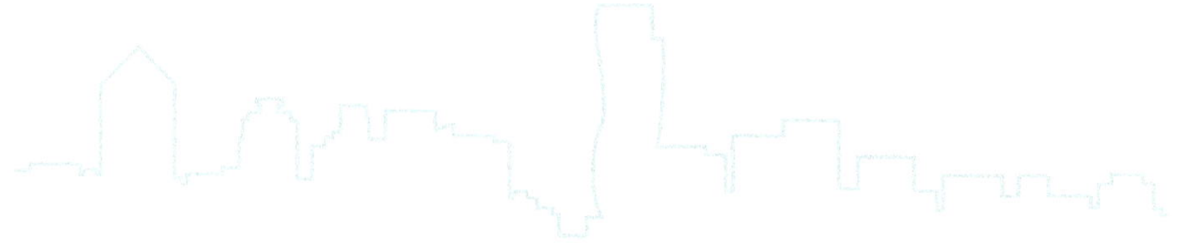

LIVING WITH LIGHT: COMMUNITY

Rikin Patel

Both of the following pieces are reflections of why having a community was so important in helping me become who I am today. The incorporations of lights contrasting against the dark background of the picture represents my struggle migrating to Canada with nothing to my family's name and no place to call home. It was a rough move as I had left all my friends, other family and other things that I had loved. Afterwards, we had moved to a suburb area in Mississauga. Our neighbourhood was an old fashioned one; where all the neighbours knew each other and allowed us to become more comfortable in settling where we were. I had made new friends, and they did an excellent job at making us feel right at home. I also started picking up hobbies here and there from them such as art and design. The lights in the pictures represent the hope and possibilities of new found friendships; something to escape the darkness that comes from losing everything. Besides yearning for a passion and instilling creativity, I have gained a sense of home and welcomeness through the people I have met within my community.

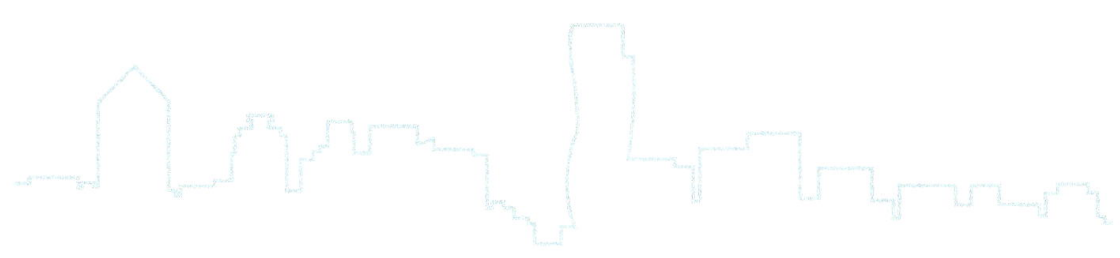

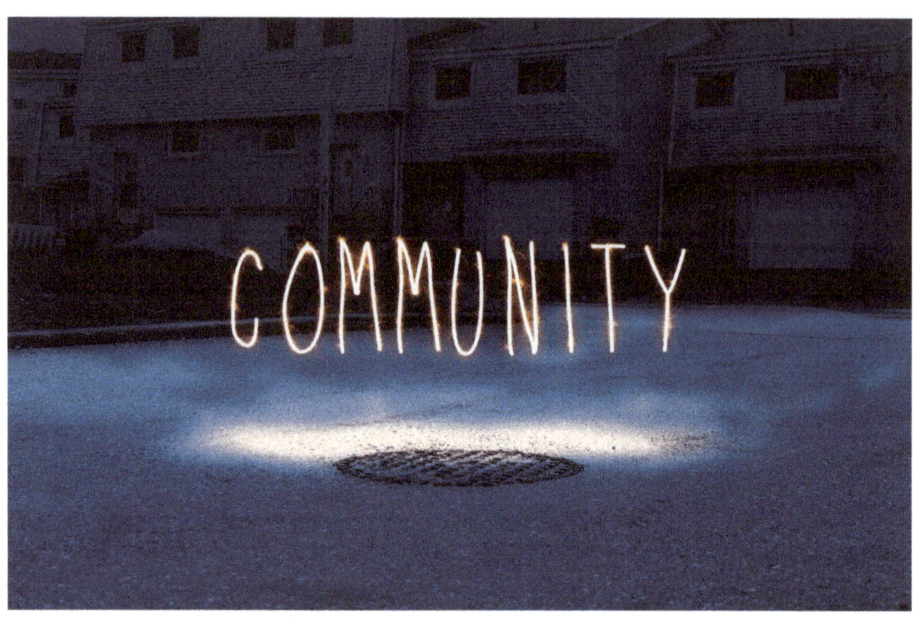
COMMUNITY

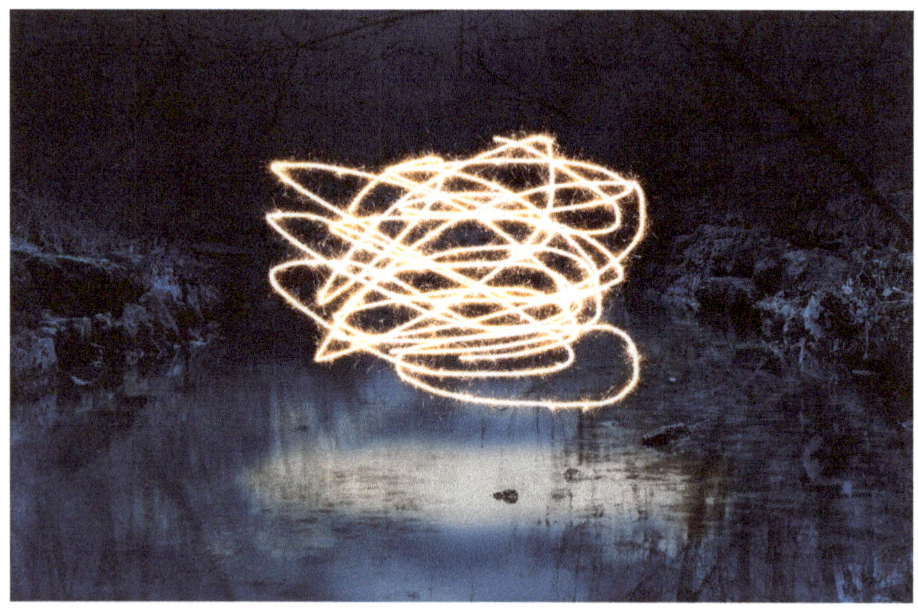

On behalf of our Ward Councillors

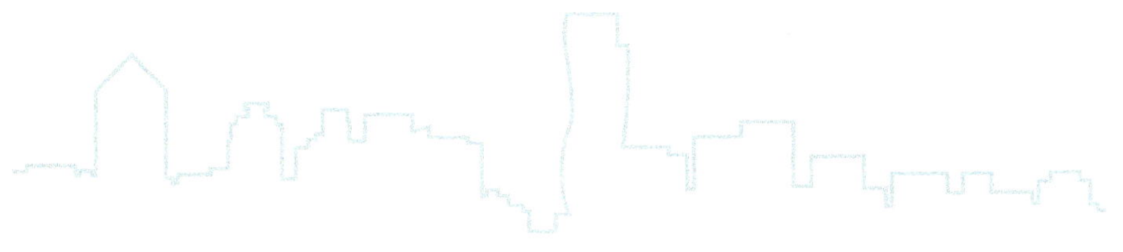

COUNCILLOR JOHN KOVAC

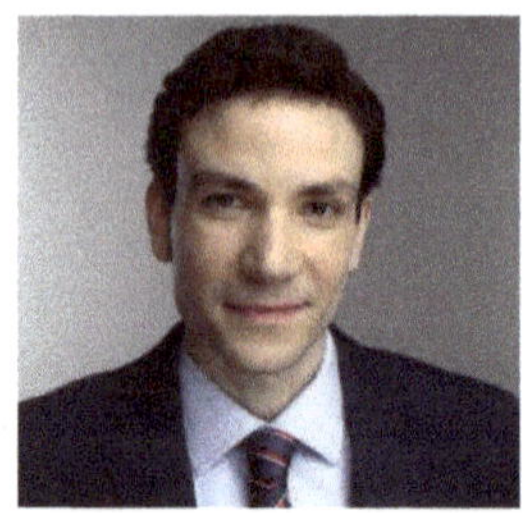

What is the importance of youth in the community and/or in the arts?

"Mississauga is a youth-friendly city that is respectful, inclusive and forward thinking; a city where youth are meaningfully engaged and thrive as equal members of our community. The City of Mississauga has a Youth Plan, officially endorsed and supported by City Council in 2009. The Youth Plan doesn't sit on a shelf! It has been used to forge over 250 partnerships with schools, churches and youth serving agencies to deliver and connect with and support youth in our community. This is one of the main reasons why, in March, 2017, the City received platinum status as a Youth Friendly Community from Play Works.

Mississauga provides important programs, services and facilities that are helping young people further develop as informed, engaged and responsible citizens. Youth-friendly spaces like Celebration Square offer lots to do year-round ranging from free concerts, outdoor movie nights, fitness and yoga classes, skating and open mic nights. The City also offers hundreds of no cost drop in youth programs each year at our libraries and community centres and has seen increasing participation numbers over the last few years. These programs include the annual Rebel campaign which empowers youth to get involved and make a difference within their community through music, film, the arts, culture and sport. In turn, we are seeing an increase in youth volunteer hours, increased youth engagement and more opportunities for mentorship.

Mississauga is home to smart, hardworking, compassionate and dynamic youth. I encourage young Mississauga residents to step up, get involved, showcase their immense talents and utilize the City programs, services and facilities to reach higher and be active, engaged and complete citizens."

COUNCILLOR GEORGE CARLSON

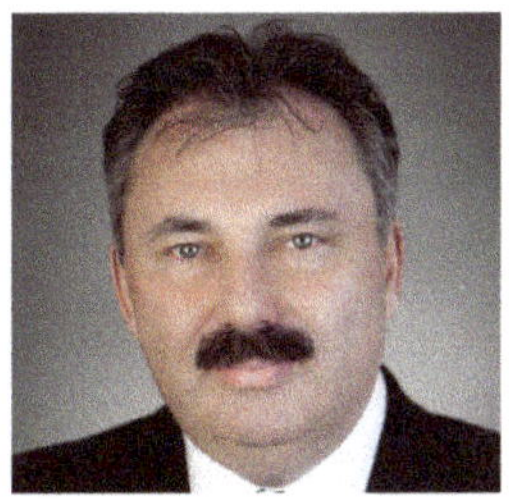

"It's exciting to be young and living in Mississauga! Our youth bring so much energy, enthusiasm, and a fresh perspective to everything that they do: they are the future of our City and our country.

Youth are the leaders and shapers of tomorrow and are vital to the success of our City and country. The City of Mississauga values our youth and is committed to being a City that is responsive to the needs and interests of youth and where youth are meaningfully engaged and can thrive in everything that they do. The City recently received platinum status as a Youth Friendly Community, where young people are enjoying an unrivalled quality of life in their own neighbourhoods, and will continue to develop and provide important programs, services, and facilities that will help young people further develop as informed, engaged, and responsible citizens."

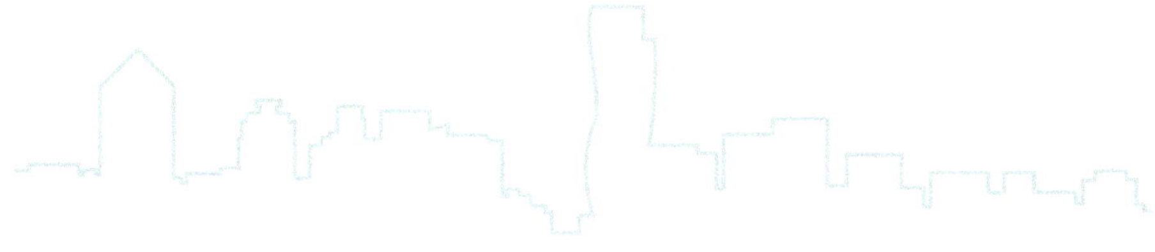

Getting involved in the community

Organizations making a difference in our community

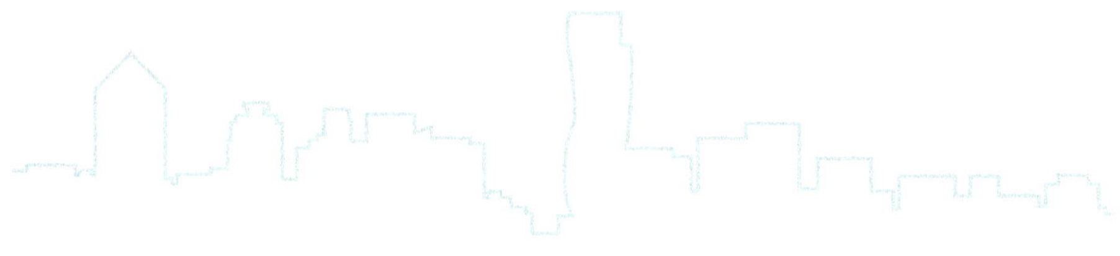

JUNIOR CHAMBER INTERNATIONAL (JCI)

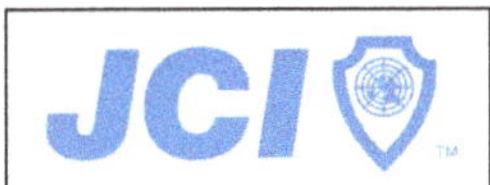

JCI IS A MEMBERSHIP-BASED NONPROFIT ORGANIZATION of young active citizens ages 18 to 40 in over 120 countries who are dedicated to creating sustainable impact in their communities. Our purpose is to provide development opportunities that empower young people to create positive change. Our members identify the problems in their communities and take action to provide sustainable solutions to these problems.

JCI launched the Global Youth Empowerment Fund as an initiative to empower young people around the world to impact their communities by investing in grassroots, community projects. As such, the Fund provided a grant to Ink Movement Mississauga in order to support their efforts at empowering young artists to engage in community development issues in connection to the Global Goals for Sustainable Development. The future unquestionably lies in the hands of young people and therefore it is imperative to empower them to be active citizens in our communities and through the arts. Young people can be involved with JCI by becoming a member at the local level, conducting a project funded by the Global Youth Empowerment Fund or simply by being an active citizen in their own community.

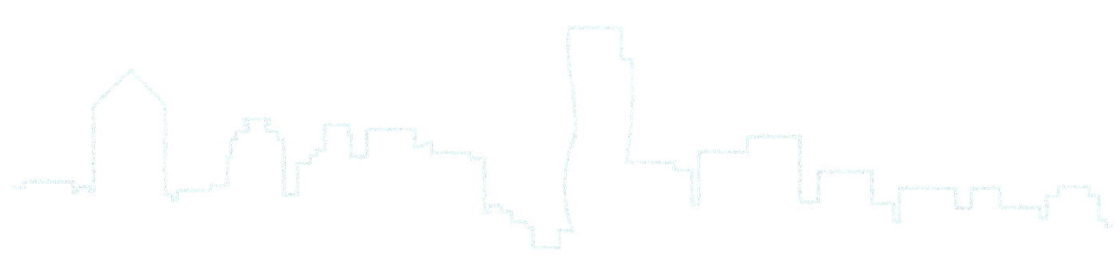

MIWAY

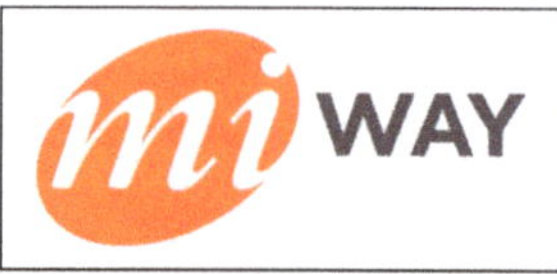

TO EXPLORE THE COMMUNITY, youth need a way to get around independently. They can walk, cycle or if they want to discover more places in Mississauga, as well as other communities they can take public transit. MiWay is the City of Mississauga's public transit service and the third largest in Ontario and an easy way to connect to Toronto, Oakville, and Brampton. MiWay provides two types of service: MiExpress for express travel on blue buses servicing limited-stop routes, and MiLocal for local travel on orange buses along regular and school routes.

High school students can get involved with MiWay by applying to be a MiWay Student Ambassador for their school. This fun and creative program provides a great opportunity for the Ambassador team to educate other students in their school about the benefits of public transit. In this program students earn community volunteer hours and have a chance to win awesome prizes including free transit for a year. One of the optional challenges in the program is to design a bus wrap. The winning bus wrap design will be on a MiWay bus that travels throughout Mississauga for one year. What a great way to display creative talent for the whole community to see!

For youth 12 – 14 years of age, MiWay offers the Freedom Pass. Youth can travel free on all MiWay buses from July 1 to August 31 and also swim free at any City of Mississauga Community pool. For more information visit www.mississauga.ca/freedompass

MiWay provides safe, independent travel to wherever youth need to be. Check us out at www.miway.ca/students or for more information about the MiWay Student Ambassador program visit https://www.facebook.com/MiWayStudentAmbassadorProgram.

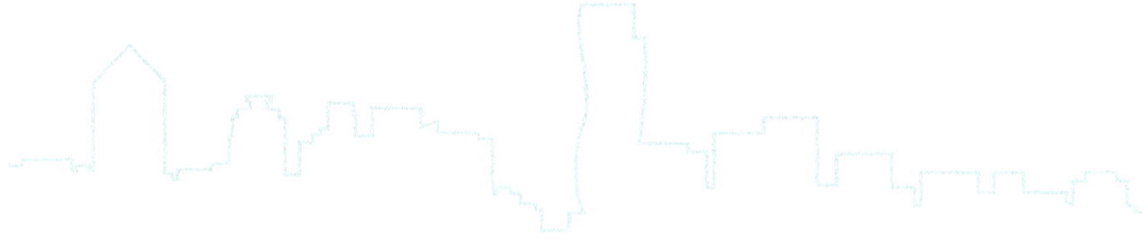

CIPHER

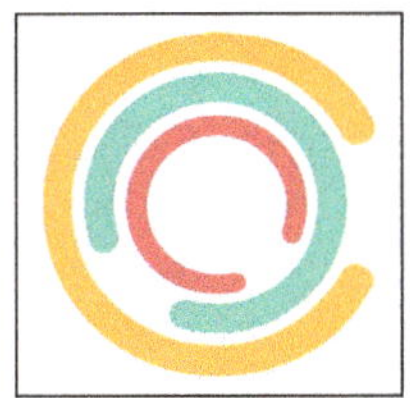

CIPHER IS A LAUNCHPAD INTO CODE for high schoolers. The compelling aspect of coding is that your interests, whether it be art or video games, play an important role in how and what you code. Everyone builds and solves problems distinctively because of their unique experiences, youth having especially interesting perspectives.

Find us at @projectcipher on social media and *projectcipher.io.*

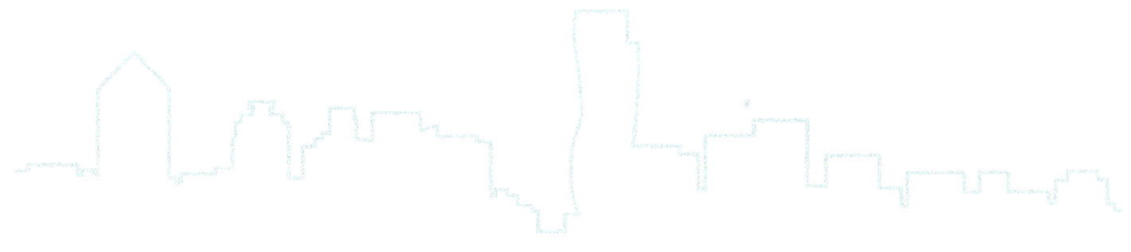

VOLUNTEER MBC

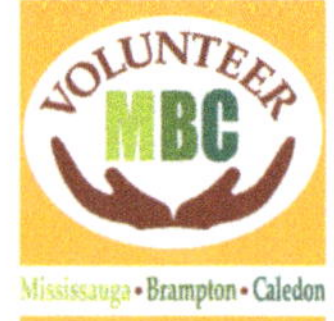

VOLUNTEER MBC'S MISSION is to "promote and support volunteerism in an effort to connect all people to meaningful volunteer opportunities in the community." Each ambassador plays an important role in their part to contribute to this mission by working towards increasing the number of student volunteers all throughout the Peel Region (Mississauga, Brampton and Caledon). We collaborate with elementary students, high school students, post-secondary students, youth lead groups and organizations, youth focused groups and organizations, and community service organizations, to make a difference in the community.

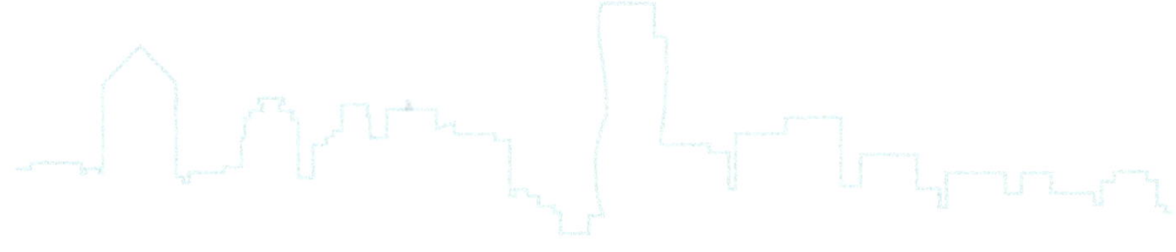

RED CROSS (IHPYC)

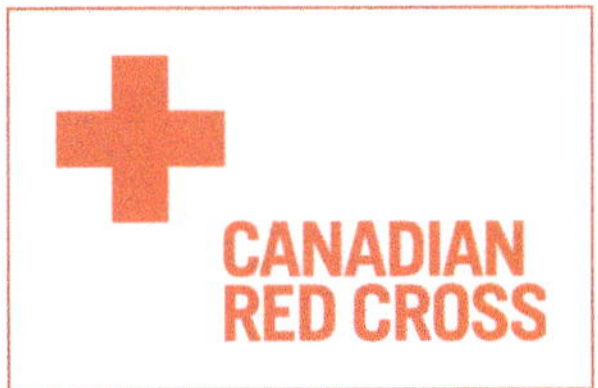

THE INTERNATIONAL HUMANITARIAN PEEL YOUTH COUNCIL (IHPYC) is an active youth organization that hosts interactive social events throughout the year to raise money for various Canadian Red Cross initiatives, while also raising awareness about the causes to students across Peel. Winterluxe and Palais Royale are two long standing and extremely popular events that the IHPYC hosts every year, both which draw in hundreds of students and raise lots of money for Red Cross initiatives. In addition to these two high-energy events, the IHPYC hosts General Meetings, with the primary goal of spreading awareness and increasing knowledge on the very causes the events are supporting.

As they say, youth are the future. By educating and engaging youth now, especially in pressing global and social issues, our community will stand a better chance at a more positive future. Based on this very principle, the IHPYC strives to spread awareness that not only has immediate gratifications, but has the potential to lead to a greater global impact.

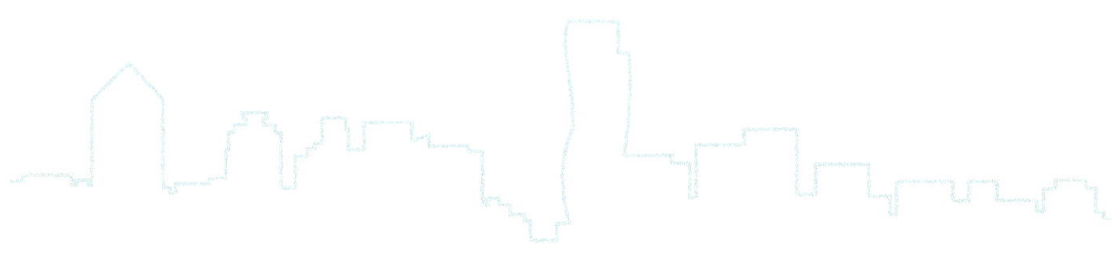

PSPC

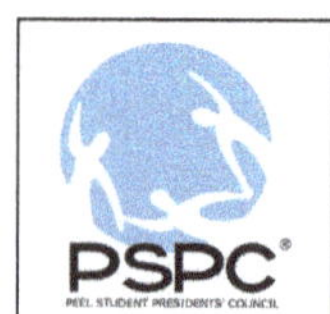

THE PEEL STUDENT PRESIDENT'S COUNCIL is an independent youth-led organization that works in harmony with the Peel District School Board to provide its students a multitude of leadership opportunities.

The PSPC strives to develop student leaders within the Peel District by providing them with opportunities to get involved within their local community. We hold several different events throughout the year to help influence student leadership as well as help students to network, collaborate and learn from one another.

Every month, we have our General Meetings at the HJA Brown Center where students can come out to learn how to be stronger leaders, collaborate with other young leaders like themselves and network with tons of new people! The General Meetings are a great way to start getting involved with the PSPC.

We also hold our Student Senate in October. This event is specifically for SAC students and is broken into two workshops. Each workshop helps develop leadership qualities that are extremely beneficial to SAC students and developing their abilities to plan exciting events and collaborate!

Furthermore, we have our annual Spring Conference! The conference is usually a 3 night/4 day trip where delegates run through sessions such as Trust and Risk or Digital Citizenship and learn how to become more well rounded individuals. The conference as a whole focuses on developing the crucial softcore skills which are needed for students to succeed worldwide.

Lastly, we have our Semi Formal! This event is an event solely designed for the students of Peel to come out, dance and enjoy themselves! It's the perfect time to have fun with your friends and meet tons of new people! The event is open to all Peel students and is always a ton of fun!

The PSPC has existed for over a decade and we will continue to work hard to help develop powerful student leaders and help the different SACs to collaborate and work together to improve all the schools in Peel!

MYAC

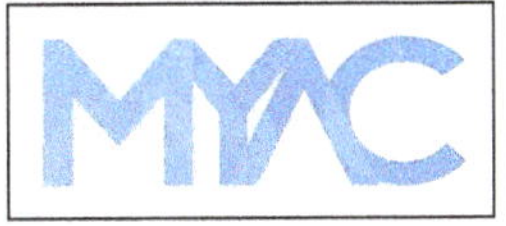

MYAC IS A PURELY YOUTH LED ORGANIZATION that is a testament to youth engagement. MYAC strives to be a dynamic, outgoing volunteer organization which spearheads a host of beneficial community projects, actively encourages youth involvement and creates unique, constructive recommendations, while aspiring to foster a positive image for the City of Mississauga and its young citizens.

MYAC hosts monthly general meetings ("Connects") that are a forum to meet new people, learn about and discuss issues affecting young people, and receive opportunities to make a difference in the community. Each Connect hosts a different yet relevant theme for the youth of Mississauga for instance Mental Health Awareness, Social Entrepreneurship, Healthy Living etc. These Connects are the foundation of our involvement within the city and is how we spread our message of youth engagement.

Our vision as a council is fairly simple and straightforward: to continue consulting youth in all pockets of Mississauga to collectively determine the voice and vision of youth across Mississauga, act as an advisory body to the City of Mississauga and to the Members of Council on all issues which pertain to youth, to provide resources and professional development to any youth in the city, to actively unite and engage various community stakeholders who have a direct impact on the youth of Mississauga, and to continue to provide volunteer opportunities to the youth.

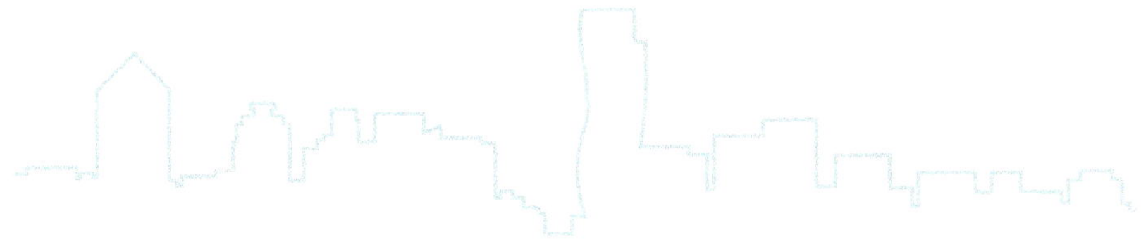

VOLUNTEERING PEEL

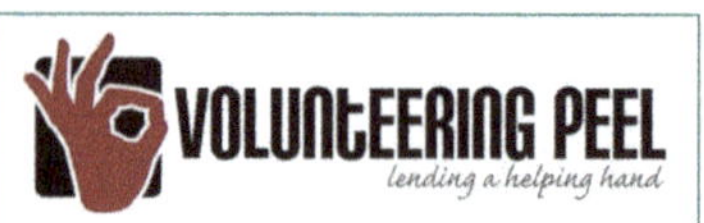

THE INVOLVEMENT and significance of youth in the community cannot be stressed enough. By being involved in the community, youth get to the opportunity to learn by example and then go on to talking on leadership roles in those respective areas. First-hand experience is vital to success in any field. Moreover, by getting involved youth get the opportunity to gain exposure to new experiences. At times, these new experiences allow them to gain a better understanding of the future career they would like to pursue. Along with the experience, youth get to make new friends and better understand their community. They are able to contribute to the greater cause of the community and contribute to a bigger picture.

Additionally, the involvement of youth in the community and arts allows the youth to express their hobbies, opinions and passion to others and spread the joy and knowledge of it. Youth are able to contribute to the community through various ways including; volunteering, getting a job or joining executive teams to assist in organizing. Without the involvement of youth, youth would be demotivated, there would be lack of development and lack of expression. All in all, today's youth are the future leaders of tomorrow and their involvement in the community is vital to personal and societal development.

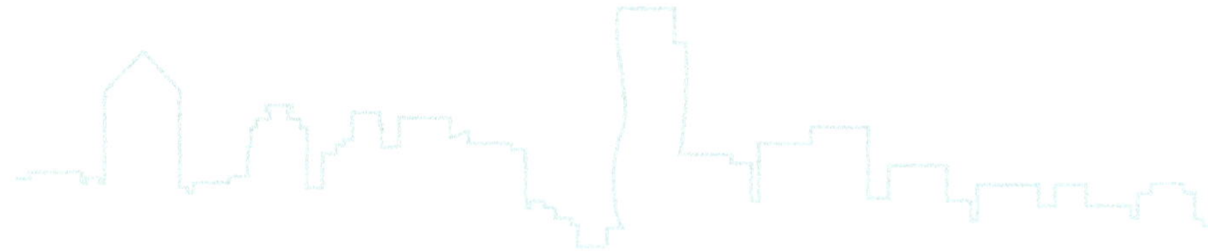

ART GALLERY OF MISSISSAUGA (AGM)

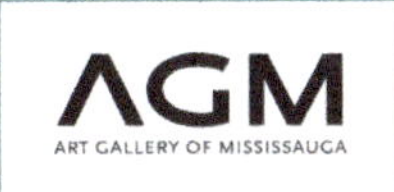

THE ART GALLERY OF MISSISSAUGA (AGM) is a public, not-for-profit art gallery located in the Mississauga Civic Centre, right on Celebration Square and across from Square One Shopping Centre. The AGM presents a changing calendar of engaging contemporary art exhibitions, featuring regional, national and international artists. As a public gallery with a strong community connection, the AGM is interested in assisting visitors as they learn about art. Projects that engage our community and reflect our awareness of contemporary and relevant cultural topics and issues are of particular interest. The gallery offers a wide range of tours, talks, and workshops for adult learners, as well as innovative youth programmes for schools, universities and community groups.

The AGM believes in supporting the NEXT generation of artists in the Mississauga community by providing diverse opportunities for engagement with the arts. Whether through collaborative curatorial projects, arts education initiatives, or volunteering, the AGM aims to empower and integrate the creative voices of youth in the community.

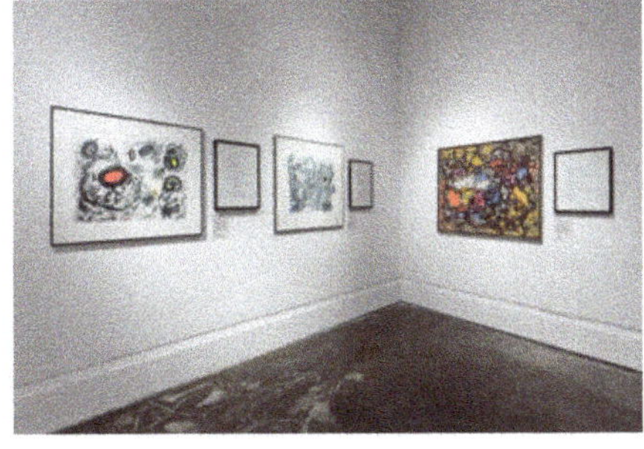

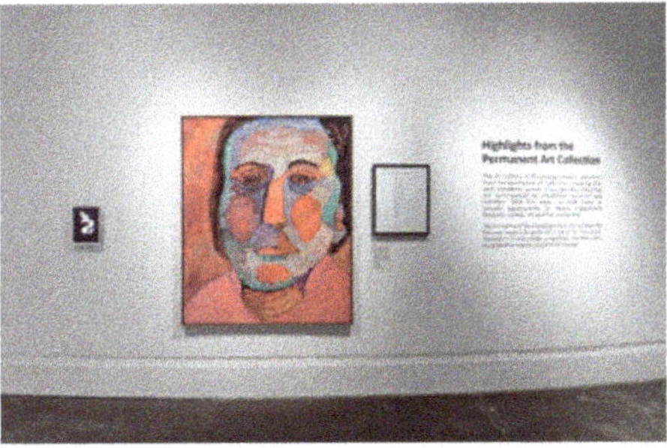

Image credit: Installation view of Art of Words | Words of Art. Photos: Toni Hafkenscheid

Art of Words | Words of Art, a permanent art collection (PAC) intervention, grew out of the longstanding relationship between the AGM and Ink Movement – Mississauga Chapter. Four participants from this year's Ink Movement Youth Anthology competition were asked to engage with the AGM's collection and select a work that best reflected or spoke to their submitted piece of poetry or prose. The resulting exhibition displayed their written works alongside their selected PAC work with a brief description on the youth participant, their writing, and the AGM artwork. The visual and verbal dialogues created between the two forms of artistic expression reveal that the creative mind has no limits in the connections it can make, and that interpretation is in the eye of the beholder.

From over 65 submissions, the top written works were selected based on theme, language, impact and originality. The following four youth participants – Jordan Currie, Diya Jhuti, Abirami Sudharshan and Sonya Zhang – submitted outstanding work and were selected to participate in the AGM's PAC intervention.

ACKNOWLEDGMENTS

The Mississauga Youth Anthology: Volume V would not have been possible without the contributions of our generous community partners and dedicated Ink Movement family!

Thank you to the Global Youth Empowerment fund for supporting this year's project; to the Art Gallery of Mississauga for their continuous support through Ink movement's initiatives, to Cheryl Antao-Xavier and her team at In Our Words Inc. for publishing the anthology, and finally, to our community supporters for making the anthology a great success!

Thank you to this year's amazing Ink Movement 2016-2017 team: Prapthi Agarwala, Kiranpreet Walia, Rehan Jay Manickam, Pujita Verma, Tahreem Alvi, Sally Co, Gracie Xia, Kim Nguyen, Jan Ly, Grace Kuang, Rana Al-Fayez, Denise Bu, Andreea Varlan, Connie Yang, Sonya Zhang, and Aleeza Qayyum. Once again, I'd like to thank our editors—Olga Nova, Khalisa Valani, and Komal Patel for their time and dedication to brainstorming and editing the anthology. Last but not least, thank you to Maxwell Tran for his extended support throughout the entire process and for creating an outlet of self-expression for the amazing youth in our community.

Sincerely,
Jacqueline Shi, Anthology Lead
Uswa Zahoor, President

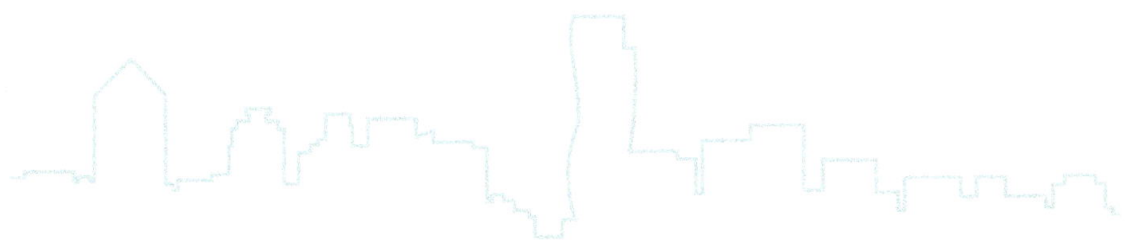

www.ingramcontent.com/pod-product-compliance
Lightning Source LLC
Chambersburg PA
CBHW040729070726
47599CB00033B/1348

* 9 7 8 1 9 2 6 9 2 6 8 3 4 *